Tefal EasyFry & Grill Air Fryer Cookbook 2024

1200 Days Delicious, Quick and No-Stress Air Fryer Recipes to Easy Fry, Grill, Roast and Bake

Denise K. Platt

CONTENTS

Fish And Seafood Recipes 41

Vegetarians Recipes 52

Poultry Recipes 65

Sandwiches And Burgers Recipes **76**

Desserts And Sweets Recipes 87

APPENDIX A: Measurement 100

APPENDIX B: Recipes Index 102

INTRODUCTION

Hello, I'm Denise K. Platt, and I am thrilled to introduce you to my Tefal Air Fryer Cookbook. With a background in culinary arts and years of experience as a professional chef, my passion for creating delicious and wholesome meals has driven me to craft a cookbook tailored specifically for Tefal Air Fryer enthusiasts.

My journey as a chef has taken me through bustling kitchens and culinary adventures, but my heart has always been dedicated to making cooking accessible and enjoyable for everyone. This cookbook is an embodiment of that dedication, and it's designed to help you make the most of your Tefal Air Fryer while creating delightful dishes in the comfort of your own home.

The core purpose of this cookbook is to provide you with a treasure trove of recipes that not only tantalize your taste buds but also simplify the cooking process. Inside, you'll find step-by-step instructions for every recipe, ensuring that whether you're a seasoned home chef or a cooking novice, you'll be able to create impressive dishes with ease.

But that's not all—my Tefal Air Fryer Cookbook goes the extra mile by offering practical cooking tips, estimated cooking times, and shopping lists for each recipe. I understand that your time is valuable, and your kitchen should be a place of culinary delight, not stress. These features help you streamline your meal planning, execution, and overall cooking experience.

Within these pages, you'll discover a diverse array of recipes, from crispy snacks and appetizers to hearty main courses and mouthwatering desserts, all designed to make the most of your Tefal Air Fryer. I firmly believe that cooking should be a joyful and rewarding experience, and this cookbook is your companion on that culinary journey.

So, whether you're a Tefal Air Fryer aficionado or just beginning to explore the world of air frying, my Tefal Air Fryer Cookbook is here to guide you. Let's embark on a flavorful and practical culinary adventure together, one delicious recipe at a time.

WHAT IS A TEFAL AIR FRYER?

The Tefal EasyFry & Grill Air Fryer is a kitchen appliance designed to provide versatile cooking options, combining the features of an air fryer and a grill in one device. Tefal is a well-known brand in the field of kitchen appliances, and their EasyFry & Grill Air Fryer is part of their range of air fryers designed to offer healthier cooking alternatives.

Air Frying: Like traditional air fryers, this appliance uses hot air circulation to cook food. It allows you to cook dishes with a crispy texture using significantly less oil compared to deep frying. This promotes healthier eating by reducing fat and calorie content in your meals.

Grilling Function: In addition to air frying, this device has a grill function. This means you can also grill items like chicken, steaks, vegetables, and more, giving your food that classic grilled flavor and appearance.

Versatility: The combination of air frying and grilling functions provides versatility in your cooking. You can prepare a wide range of dishes, from fried favorites like French fries and chicken wings to grilled meats and vegetables.

WHAT ARE THE BENEFITS OF AIR FRYER COOKING?

Healthier Cooking

Air fryers use hot air circulation to cook food, requiring significantly less oil than traditional deep frying. This results in meals that are lower in unhealthy fats and calories, making it a healthier option for those conscious of their diet.

Reduced Risk of Health Issues

Lower oil consumption can contribute to a reduced risk of obesity, heart disease, and other health issues associated with excessive fat intake.

Crispy Texture

Air fryers can achieve a crispy and crunchy texture similar to deep-fried foods without the need for excessive oil. This allows you to enjoy crispy snacks and treats with fewer calories.

Faster Cooking

Air fryers cook food faster than traditional ovens, which is convenient for busy individuals and families. It helps you get meals on the table more quickly.

Versatility

Air fryers are versatile and can cook a wide range of foods, including vegetables, meats, seafood, and even desserts. You can prepare a variety of dishes using a single appliance.

Easy Cleanup

Many air fryer baskets and trays are non-stick and dishwasher-safe, making cleanup quick and hassle-free.

Less Mess

Air fryers are less messy compared to deep frying because there is no hot oil to splatter or dispose of.

AIR FRYER COOKING TIPS

1. Preheat your Air Fryer…well, most of the time

It's common practice that any cooking element should be preheated. Most brands of air fryers specify that the air fryer should be preheated to ensure even cooking. I do it sometimes, other times I don't and my food still turns out delicious. If your air fryer does not have a preheat setting, simply turn it to the desired temperature and allow it to run for around 3 minutes before placing your food in.

2. Use oil on your foods for the air fryer…well, most of the time

I like to use oil on certain foods to help them crisp but certain foods don't necessarily need it. If your food already has some fat on it (dark meat chicken, ground beef, fatty cuts of meat, etc.) then you probably don't need the oil. I use oil on vegetables (like my Breakfast Air Fried Potatoes) and any battered seafood, !like my Crispy Air Fryer Fish).

3. Grease your Air Fryer Basket

Even if your food does not require oil, always take a moment to at least grease your air fryer basket. I grease mine by rubbing, or spraying, a little bit of oil on the bottom grates. This will ensure that your food won't stick.

4. Don't overcrowd the basket

If you want your fried foods to turn out crispy, you'll want to make sure you don't overcrowd the basket. Placing too much food in the basket will prevent your food from crisping and browning. To ensure this doesn't happen, cook your food in batches or invest in a bigger air fryer.

5. Shake the basket during cooking for fries, wings, etc.

When air frying smaller items, like chicken wings, french fries, and similar items, you'll want to shake the basket every few minutes to ensure even cooking. Sometimes I use a pair of silicone kitchen tongs to flip larger items over rather than shaking. Once you open the basket to shake, the air fryer will temporarily pause but will resume cooking your food at the same temperature once you return the basket.

6. Spray halfway through cooking

I found that spraying with oil halfway through cooking gets the best crisp on most foods. I tend to wait and spray halfway through cooking unless it's an item that doesn't need spraying, like fatty meats. Coated food items should be sprayed. Also, spray any dry flour spots that still appear halfway through air frying.

7. Adjust the Temperature for Certain Foods

It can sometimes be tempting to crank the heat for the Air Fryer to the highest temp to let it run but be careful as some foods can dry out quickly. A good rule of thumb is to modify the temperature and time from how long you would typically make it in the oven. I like to go 30 degrees below and cut the time by about 20%. For example, if you cooked brownies at 350 degrees Fahrenheit for 20 minutes in the oven, cut the degrees on the Air Fryer to 320 degrees and cook for about 16 minutes.

HOW TO CLEAN YOUR TEFAL AIR FRYER?

Materials You'll Need:

Warm, soapy water

Soft sponge or cloth

Non-abrasive brush

Dishwashing liquid

Soft-bristle brush or toothbrush

Clean, dry cloth or paper towels

Instructions:

- Make sure the air fryer is unplugged and cooled down before you begin cleaning.

- Depending on the model of your Tefal Air Fryer, there may be some removable parts such as baskets, drawers and trays. Please remove these parts carefully.

- Empty any food crumbs or residue from baskets, drawers and trays into the trash.

- Soak removable parts in warm soapy water. Soak for about 10-15 minutes. Wipe the inside of the air fryer with a soft sponge or cloth to remove loose food particles.

- Clean Heating Element: The heating element on top of the air fryer can accumulate grease and debris. Wipe the outside of the air fryer with a damp cloth to remove any splatters or spills. Avoid getting water into the vents or control panel.

- After soaking, thoroughly clean removable parts with a soft sponge or brush. Note any stubborn spots and scrub gently with a brush or toothbrush.

- Rinse all parts under running water to remove soap residue. Ensure that it is completely dry before reassembling. Pat dry with a clean, dry cloth or paper towel if necessary.

Breakfast & Snacks And Fries Recipes

Loaded Hash Browns

Servings: 4
Cooking Time:xx
Ingredients:

- 4 large potatoes
- 2 tbsp bicarbonate of soda
- 1 tbsp salt
- 1 tbsp black pepper
- 1 tsp cayenne pepper
- 2 tbsp olive oil
- 1 large chopped onion
- 1 chopped red pepper
- 1 chopped green pepper

Directions:

1. Grate the potatoes
2. Squeeze out any water contained within the potatoes
3. Take a large bowl of water and add the potatoes
4. Add the bicarbonate of soda, combine everything and leave to soak for 25 minutes
5. Drain the water away and carefully pat the potatoes to dry
6. Transfer your potatoes into another bowl
7. Add the spices and oil
8. Combining everything well, tossing to coat evenly
9. Place your potatoes into your fryer basket
10. Set to 200ºC and cook for 10 minutes
11. Give the potatoes a shake and add the peppers and the onions
12. Cook for another 10 minutes

Meaty Egg Cups

Servings: 4
Cooking Time:xx
Ingredients:

- 8 slices of toasted sandwich bread
- 2 slices of ham
- 4 eggs
- Salt and pepper to taste
- Butter for greasing

Directions:

1. Take 4 ramekins and grease the insides with a little butter
2. Flatten the slices of toast with a rolling pin and arrange inside the ramekins - two in each
3. Line the inside of each ramekin with a slice of ham
4. Crack one egg into each ramekin
5. Season with a little salt and pepper
6. Place the ramekins into the air fryer and cook at 160ºC for 15 minutes
7. Remove from the fryer and wait to cool just slightly
8. Remove and serve

Breakfast Sausage Burgers

Servings: 2
Cooking Time:xx
Ingredients:

- 8 links of your favourite sausage
- Salt and pepper to taste

Directions:

1. Remove the sausage from the skins and use a fork to create a smooth mixture
2. Season to your liking
3. Shape the sausage mixture into burgers or patties
4. Preheat your air fryer to 260ºC
5. Arrange the burgers in the fryer, so they are not touching each other
6. Cook for 8 minutes
7. Serve still warm

Blanket Breakfast Eggs

Servings: 2
Cooking Time:xx
Ingredients:

- 2 eggs
- 2 slices of sandwich bread
- Olive oil spray
- Salt and pepper to taste

Directions:

1. Preheat your air fryer to 190ºC and spray with a little oil
2. Meanwhile, take your bread and cut a hole into the middle of each piece
3. Place one slice inside your fryer and crack one egg into the middle
4. Season with a little salt and pepper

5. Cook for 5 minutes, before turning over and cooking for a further 2 minutes

6. Remove the first slice and repeat the process with the remaining slice of bread and egg

Your Favourite Breakfast Bacon

Servings: 2

Cooking Time:xx

Ingredients:

- 4-5 rashers of lean bacon, fat cut off
- Salt and pepper for seasoning

Directions:

1. Line your air fryer basket with parchment paper
2. Place the bacon in the basket
3. Set the fryer to 200°C
4. Cook for 10 minutes for crispy. If you want it very crispy, cook for another 2 minutes

Avocado Fries

Servings: 2

Cooking Time:xx

Ingredients:

- 35 g/¼ cup plain/all-purpose flour (gluten free if you wish)
- ½ teaspoon chilli/chili powder
- 1 egg, beaten
- 50 g/heaped ½ cup dried breadcrumbs (gluten-free if you wish; see page 9)
- 1 avocado, skin and stone removed, and each half sliced lengthways
- salt and freshly ground black pepper

Directions:

1. Preheat the air-fryer to 200°C/400°F.
2. In a bowl combine the flour and chilli/chili powder, then season with salt and pepper. Place the beaten egg in a second bowl and the breadcrumbs in a third bowl.
3. Dip each avocado slice in the seasoned flour (shaking off any excess), then the egg and finally the breadcrumbs.
4. Add the breaded avocado slices to the preheated air-fryer and air-fry for 6 minutes, turning after 4 minutes. Serve immediately.

Morning Sausage Wraps

Servings: 8

Cooking Time:xx

Ingredients:

- 8 sausages, chopped into pieces
- 2 slices of cheddar cheese, cut into quarters
- 1 can of regular crescent roll dough
- 8 wooden skewers

Directions:

1. Take the dough and separate each one
2. Cut open the sausages evenly
3. The one of your crescent rolls and on the widest part, add a little sausage and then a little cheese
4. Roll the dough and tuck it until you form a triangle
5. Repeat this for four times and add into your air fryer
6. Cook at 190°C for 3 minutes
7. Remove your dough and add a skewer for serving
8. Repeat with the other four pieces of dough

Bocconcini Balls

Servings: 2

Cooking Time:xx

Ingredients:

- 70 g/½ cup plus ½ tablespoon plain/all-purpose flour (gluten-free if you wish)
- 1 egg, beaten
- 70 g/1 cup dried breadcrumbs (gluten-free if you wish; see page 9)
- 10 bocconcini

Directions:

1. Preheat the air-fryer to 200°C/400°F.
2. Place the flour, egg and breadcrumbs on 3 separate plates. Dip each bocconcini ball first in the flour to coat, then the egg, shaking off any excess before rolling in the breadcrumbs.
3. Add the breaded bocconcini to the preheated air-fryer and air-fry for 5 minutes (no need to turn them during cooking). Serve immediately.

Baba Ganoush

Servings: 4

Cooking Time:xx

Ingredients:

- 1 large aubergine/eggplant, sliced in half lengthways
- ½ teaspoon salt
- 5 tablespoons olive oil
- 1 bulb garlic
- 30 g/2 tablespoons tahini or nut butter
- 2 tablespoons freshly squeezed lemon juice
- ½ teaspoon ground cumin

- ¼ teaspoon smoked paprika
- salt and freshly ground black pepper
- 3 tablespoons freshly chopped flat-leaf parsley

Directions:

1. Preheat the air-fryer to 200°C/400°F.

2. Lay the aubergine/eggplant halves cut side up. Sprinkle over the salt, then drizzle over 1 tablespoon of oil. Cut the top off the garlic bulb, brush the exposed cloves with a little olive oil, then wrap in foil. Place the aubergine/eggplant and foil-wrapped garlic in the preheated air-fryer and air-fry for 15–20 minutes until the inside of the aubergine is soft and buttery in texture.

3. Scoop the flesh of the aubergine into a bowl. Squeeze out about 1 tablespoon of the cooked garlic and add to the bowl with the remaining 4 tablespoons of olive oil, the tahini/nut butter, lemon juice, spices and salt and pepper to taste. Mix well and serve with fresh flat-leaf parsley sprinkled over.

Toad In The Hole, Breakfast Style

Servings: 4
Cooking Time:xx

Ingredients:

- 1 sheet of puff pastry (defrosted)
- 4 eggs
- 4 tbsp grated cheese (cheddar works well)
- 4 slices of cooked ham, cut into pieces
- Chopped fresh herbs of your choice

Directions:

1. Preheat your air fryer to 200°C

2. Take your pastry sheet and place it on a flat surface, cutting it into four pieces

3. Take two of the pastry sheets and place them inside your fryer, cooking for up to 8 minutes, until done

4. Remove the pastry and flatten the centre down with a spoon, to form a deep hole

5. Add a tablespoon of the cheese and a tablespoon of the ham into the hole

6. Crack one egg into the hole

7. Return the pastry to the air fryer and cook for another 6 minutes, or until the egg is done as you like it

8. Remove and allow to cool

9. Repeat the process with the rest of the pastry remaining

10. Sprinkle fresh herbs on top and serve

Courgette Fries

Servings: 2
Cooking Time:xx

Ingredients:

- 1 courgette/zucchini
- 3 tablespoons plain/all-purpose flour (gluten-free if you wish)
- ¼ teaspoon salt
- ¼ teaspoon freshly ground black pepper
- 60 g/¾ cup dried breadcrumbs (gluten-free if you wish; see page 9)
- 1 teaspoon dried oregano
- 20 g/¼ cup finely grated Parmesan
- 1 egg, beaten

Directions:

1. Preheat the air-fryer to 180°C/350°F.

2. Slice the courgette/zucchini into fries about 1.5 x 1.5 x 5 cm/⅝ x ⅝ x 2 in.

3. Season the flour with salt and pepper. Combine the breadcrumbs with the oregano and Parmesan.

4. Dip the courgettes/zucchini in the flour (shaking off any excess flour), then the egg, then the seasoned breadcrumbs.

5. Add the fries to the preheated air-fryer and air-fry for 15 minutes. They should be crispy on the outside but soft on the inside. Serve immediately.

Easy Cheese & Bacon Toasties

Servings: 2
Cooking Time:xx

Ingredients:

- 4 slices of sandwich bread
- 2 slices of cheddar cheese
- 5 slices of pre-cooked bacon
- 1 tbsp melted butter
- 2 slices of mozzarella cheese

Directions:

1. Take the bread and spread the butter onto one side of each slice

2. Place one slice of bread into the fryer basket, buttered side facing downwards

3. Place the cheddar on top, followed by the bacon, mozzarella and the other slice of bread on top, buttered side upwards

4. Set your fryer to 170°C

5. Cook for 4 minutes and then turn over and cook for another 3 minutes

6. Serve whilst still hot

Apple Crisps

Servings: 2
Cooking Time:xx
Ingredients:

- 2 apples, chopped
- 1 tsp cinnamon
- 2 tbsp brown sugar
- 1 tsp lemon juice
- 2.5 tbsp plain flour
- 3 tbsp oats
- 2 tbsp cold butter
- Pinch of salt

Directions:

1. Preheat the air fryer to 260ºC
2. Take a 5" baking dish and crease
3. Take a large bowl and combine the apples with the sugar, cinnamon and lemon juice
4. Add the mixture to the baking dish and cover with aluminium foil
5. Place in the air fryer and cook for 15 minutes
6. Open the lid and cook for another 5 minutes
7. Combine the rest of the ingredients in a food processor, until a crumble-type mixture occurs
8. Add over the top of the cooked apples
9. Cook with the lid open for another 5 minutes
10. Allow to cool a little before serving

French Toast

Servings: 2
Cooking Time:xx
Ingredients:

- 2 beaten eggs
- 2 tbsp softened butter
- 4 slices of sandwich bread
- 1 tsp cinnamon
- 1 tsp nutmeg
- 1 tsp ground cloves
- 1 tsp maple syrup

Directions:

1. Preheat your fryer to 180ºC

2. Take a bowl and add the eggs, salt, cinnamon, nutmeg, and cloves, combining well

3. Take your bread and butter each side, cutting into strips

4. Dip the bread slices into the egg mixture

5. Arrange each slice into the basket of your fryer

6. Cook for 2 minutes

7. Take the basket out and spray with a little cooking spray

8. Turn over the slices and place back into the fryer

9. Cook for 4 minutes

10. Remove and serve with maple syrup

Cumin Shoestring Carrots

Servings: 2
Cooking Time:xx
Ingredients:

- 300 g/10½ oz. carrots
- 1 teaspoon cornflour/cornstarch
- 1 teaspoon ground cumin
- ¼ teaspoon salt
- 1 tablespoon olive oil
- garlic mayonnaise, to serve

Directions:

1. Preheat the air-fryer to 200ºC/400ºF.
2. Peel the carrots and cut into thin fries, roughly 10 cm x 1 cm x 5 mm/4 x ½ x ¼ in. Toss the carrots in a bowl with all the other ingredients.
3. Add the carrots to the preheated air-fryer and air-fry for 9 minutes, shaking the drawer of the air-fryer a couple of times during cooking. Serve with garlic mayo on the side.

Cheesy Sausage Breakfast Pockets

Servings: 2
Cooking Time:xx
Ingredients:

- 1 packet of regular puff pastry
- 4 sausages, cooked and crumbled into pieces
- 5 eggs
- 50g cooked bacon
- 50g grated cheddar cheese

Directions:

1. Scramble your eggs in your usual way

2. Add the sausage and the bacon as you are cooking the eggs and combine well

3. Take your pastry sheets and cut rectangular shapes

4. Add a little of the egg and meat mixture to one half of each pastry piece

5. Fold the rectangles over and use a fork to seal down the edges

6. Place your pockets into your air fryer and cook at 190ºC for 10 minutes

7. Allow to cool before serving

Whole Mini Peppers

Servings: 2
Cooking Time:xx
Ingredients:
- 9 whole mini (bell) peppers
- 1 teaspoon olive oil
- ¼ teaspoon salt

Directions:
1. Preheat the air-fryer to 180ºC/350ºF.

2. Place the peppers in a baking dish that fits in for your air-fryer and drizzle over the oil, then sprinkle over the salt.

3. Add the dish to the preheated air-fryer and air-fry for 10–12 minutes, depending on how 'chargrilled' you like your peppers.

Raspberry Breakfast Pockets

Servings: 1
Cooking Time:xx
Ingredients:
- 2 slices of sandwich bread
- 1 tbsp soft cream cheese
- 1 tbsp raspberry jam
- 1 tbsp milk
- 1 egg

Directions:
1. Take one slice of the bread and add one tablespoon of jam into the middle

2. Take the second slice and add the cream cheese into the middle

3. Using a blunt knife, spread the jam and the cheese across the bread, but don't go to the outer edges

4. Take a small bowl and whisk the eggs and the milk together

5. Set your fryer to 190ºC and spray with a little oil

6. Dip your sandwich into the egg and arrange inside your fryer

7. Cook for 5 minutes on the first side, turn and cook for another 2 minutes

Crunchy Mexican Breakfast Wrap

Servings: 2
Cooking Time:xx
Ingredients:
- 2 large tortillas
- 2 corn tortillas
- 1 sliced jalapeño pepper
- 4 tbsp ranchero sauce
- 1 sliced avocado
- 25g cooked pinto beans

Directions:
1. Take each of your large tortillas and add the egg, jalapeño, sauce, the corn tortillas, the avocado and the pinto beans, in that order. If you want to add more sauce at this point, you can

2. Fold over your wrap to make sure that nothing escapes

3. Place each wrap into your fryer and cook at 190ºC for 6 minutes

4. Remove your wraps and place in the oven, cooking for a further 5 minutes at 180ºC, until crispy

5. Place each wrap into a frying pan and crisp a little more on a low heat, for a couple of minutes on each side

Oozing Baked Eggs

Servings: 2
Cooking Time:xx
Ingredients:
- 4 eggs
- 140g smoked gouda cheese, cut into small pieces
- Salt and pepper to taste

Directions:
1. You will need two ramekin dishes and spray each one before using

2. Crack two eggs into each ramekin dish

3. Add half of the Gouda cheese to each dish

4. Season and place into the air fryer

5. Cook at 350ºC for 15 minutes, until the eggs are cooked as you like them

Hard Boiled Eggs Air Fryer Style

Servings: 2
Cooking Time:xx
Ingredients:
- 4 large eggs
- 1 tsp cayenne pepper
- Salt and pepper for seasoning

Directions:
1. Preheat the air fryer to 220ºC
2. Take a wire rack and place inside the air fryer
3. Lay the eggs on the rack
4. Cook for between 15-17 minutes, depending upon how you like your eggs
5. Remove from the fryer and place in a bowl of cold water for around 5 minutes
6. Peel and season with the cayenne and the salt and pepper

Breakfast Doughnuts

Servings: 4
Cooking Time:xx
Ingredients:
- 1 packet of Pillsbury Grands
- 5 tbsp raspberry jam
- 1 tbsp melted butter
- 5 tbsp sugar

Directions:
1. Preheat your air fryer to 250ºC
2. Place the Pillsbury Grands into the air fryer and cook for around 5m minutes
3. Remove and place to one side
4. Take a large bowl and add the sugar
5. Coat the doughnuts in the melted butter, coating evenly
6. Dip into the sugar and coat evenly once more
7. Using an icing bag, add the jam into the bag and pipe an even amount into each doughnut
8. Eat warm or cold

Patatas Bravas

Servings: 4
Cooking Time:xx
Ingredients:
- 300g potatoes

- 1 tsp garlic powder
- 1 tbsp avocado oil
- 1 tbsp smoked paprika
- Salt and pepper to taste

Directions:
1. Peel the potatoes and cut them into cubes
2. Bring a large saucepan of water to the boil and add the potatoes, cooking for 6 minutes
3. Strain the potatoes and place them on a piece of kitchen towel, allowing to dry
4. Take a large mixing bowl and add the garlic powder, salt, and pepper and add the avocado oil, mixing together well
5. Add the potatoes to the bowl and coat liberally
6. Place the potatoes into the basket and arrange them with space in-between
7. Set your fryer to 200ºC
8. Cook the potatoes for 15 minutes, giving them a shake at the halfway point
9. Remove and serve

Cheese Scones

Servings:12
Cooking Time:xx
Ingredients:
- ½ teaspoon baking powder
- 210 g/1½ cups self-raising/self-rising flour (gluten-free if you wish), plus extra for dusting
- 50 g/3½ tablespoons cold butter, cubed
- 125 g/1½ cups grated mature Cheddar
- a pinch of cayenne pepper
- a pinch of salt
- 100 ml/7 tablespoons milk, plus extra for brushing the tops of the scones

Directions:
1. Mix the baking powder with the flour in a bowl, then add the butter and rub into the flour to form a crumblike texture. Add the cheese, cayenne pepper and salt and stir. Then add the milk, a little at a time, and bring together into a ball of dough.
2. Dust your work surface with flour. Roll the dough flat until about 1.5 cm/⅝ in. thick. Cut out the scones using a 6-cm/2½-in. diameter cookie cutter. Gather the offcuts into a ball, re-roll and cut more scones – you should get about 12 scones from the mixture. Place the scones on an air-fryer liner or a piece of pierced parchment paper.

3. Preheat the air-fryer to 180ºC/350ºF.

4. Add the scones to the preheated air-fryer and air-fry for 8 minutes, turning them over halfway to cook the other side. Remove and allow to cool a little, then serve warm.

Delicious Breakfast Casserole

Servings: 4
Cooking Time:xx
Ingredients:

- 4 frozen hash browns
- 8 sausages, cut into pieces
- 4 eggs
- 1 diced yellow pepper
- 1 diced green pepper
- 1 diced red pepper
- Half a diced onion

Directions:

1. Line the bottom of your fryer with aluminium foil and arrange the hash browns inside

2. Add the sausage on top (uncooked)

3. Now add the onions and the peppers, sprinkling evenly

4. Cook the casserole on 170ºC for around 10 minutes

5. Open your fryer and give the mixture a good stir

6. Combine the eggs in a small bowl and pour over the casserole, closing the lid

7. Cook for another 10 minutes on the same temperature

8. Serve with a little seasoning to taste

Breakfast Eggs & Spinach

Servings: 4
Cooking Time:xx
Ingredients:

- 500g wilted, fresh spinach
- 200g sliced deli ham
- 1 tbsp olive oil
- 4 eggs
- 4 tsp milk
- Salt and pepper to taste
- 1 tbsp butter for cooking

Directions:

1. Preheat your air fryer to 180ºC

2. You will need 4 small ramekin dishes, coated with a little butter

3. Arrange the wilted spinach, ham, 1 teaspoon of milk and 1 egg into each ramekin and season with a little salt and pepper

4. Place in the fryer 15 to 20 minutes, until the egg is cooked to your liking

5. Allow to cool before serving

Mexican Breakfast Burritos

Servings: 6
Cooking Time:xx
Ingredients:

- 6 scrambled eggs
- 6 medium tortillas
- Half a minced red pepper
- 8 sausages, cut into cubes and browned
- 4 pieces of bacon, pre-cooked and cut into pieces
- 65g grated cheese of your choice
- A small amount of olive oil for cooking

Directions:

1. Into a regular mixing bowl, combine the eggs, bell pepper, bacon pieces, the cheese, and the browned sausage, giving everything a good stir

2. Take your first tortilla and place half a cup of the mixture into the middle, folding up the top and bottom and rolling closed

3. Repeat until all your tortillas have been used

4. Arrange the burritos into the bottom of your fryer and spray with a little oil

5. Cook the burritos at 170ºC for 5 minutes

European Pancakes

Servings: 5
Cooking Time:xx
Ingredients:

- 3 large eggs
- 130g flour
- 140ml whole milk
- 2 tbsp unsweetened apple sauce
- A pinch of salt

Directions:

1. Set your fryer to 200ºC and add five ramekins inside to heat up

2. Place all your ingredients inside a blender to combine

3. Spray the ramekins with a little cooking spray

4. Pour the batter into the ramekins carefully

5. Fry for between 6-8 minutes, depending on your preference

6. Serve with your favourite toppings

Blueberry & Lemon Breakfast Muffins

Servings: 12
Cooking Time:xx

Ingredients:

- 315g self raising flour
- 65g sugar
- 120ml double cream
- 2 tbsp of light cooking oil
- 2 eggs
- 125g blueberries
- The zest and juice of a lemon
- 1 tsp vanilla

Directions:

1. Take a small bowl and mix the self raising flour and sugar together

2. Take another bowl and mix together the oil, juice, eggs, cream, and vanilla

3. Add this mixture to the flour mixture and blend together

4. Add the blueberries and fold

5. You will need individual muffin holders, silicone works best. Spoon the mixture into the holders

6. Cook at 150ºC for 10 minutes

7. Check at the halfway point to check they're not cooking too fast

8. Remove and allow to cool

French Toast Slices

Servings: 1
Cooking Time:xx

Ingredients:

- 2 eggs
- 5 slices sandwich bread

- 100ml milk
- 2 tbsp flour
- 3 tbsp sugar
- 1 tsp ground cinnamon
- 1/2 tsp vanilla extract
- Pinch of salt

Directions:

1. Preheat your air fryer to 220ºC

2. Take your bread and cut it into three pieces of the same size

3. Take a mixing bowl and combine the other ingredients until smooth

4. Dip the bread into the mixture, coating evenly

5. Take a piece of parchment paper and lay it inside the air fryer

6. Arrange the bread on the parchment paper in one layer

7. Cook for 5 minutes

8. Turn and cook for another 5 minutes

Halloumi Fries

Servings: 2
Cooking Time:xx

Ingredients:

- 225 g/8 oz. halloumi
- 40 g/heaped ¼ cup plain/all-purpose flour (gluten-free if you wish)
- ½ teaspoon sweet smoked paprika
- ½ teaspoon dried oregano
- ¼ teaspoon mild chilli/chili powder
- olive oil or avocado oil, for spraying

Directions:

1. Preheat the air-fryer to 180ºC/350ºF.

2. Slice the halloumi into fries roughly 2 x 1.5 cm/¾ x ⅝ in.

3. Mix the flour and seasoning in a bowl and dip each halloumi stick into the flour to coat. Spray with a little oil.

4. Add the fries to the preheated air-fryer and air-fry for 5 minutes. Serve immediately.

Appetizers And Snacks Recipes

Hungarian Spiralized Fries

Servings: 4
Cooking Time: 30 Minutes
Ingredients:

- 2 russet potatoes, peeled
- 15ml (1 tbsp) olive oil
- 2.5ml (½ tsp) chili powder
- 2.5ml (½ tsp) garlic powder
- 2.5ml (½ tsp) Hungarian paprika
- Salt and pepper to taste
- Instructions:
- Preheat your air fryer to 200°C (400°F).
- Using a spiralizer, cut the peeled potatoes into 12.7cm (5-inch) lengths and place them in a large bowl.
- Fill the bowl with cold water, cover it, and let the potatoes soak for 30 minutes.
- After soaking, drain the potatoes and pat them dry with a kitchen towel. Return them to the bowl.
- Drizzle the potatoes with the olive oil and season them with salt, pepper, chili powder, garlic powder, and Hungarian paprika. Toss the potatoes to ensure they are evenly coated with the seasonings.
- Place the seasoned spiralized potatoes in the air fryer basket.
- Air fry the potatoes for approximately 10-12 minutes, shaking the basket once during cooking to ensure they cook evenly. Cook until the potatoes are golden and crispy.
- Once done, remove the Hungarian Spiralized Fries from the air fryer and serve them while they are still hot.

Cinnamon Apple Crisps

Servings: 1
Cooking Time: 22 Minutes
Ingredients:

- 1 large apple
- 1.25g ground cinnamon
- 10ml avocado oil or coconut oil

Directions:

1. Preheat the air fryer to 150°C (300°F).
2. Using a mandolin or knife, slice the apples to 6mm (¼-inch) thickness.
3. Pat the apple slices dry with a paper towel or kitchen cloth.
4. Sprinkle the apple slices with ground cinnamon.
5. Spray or drizzle the oil over the top of the apple slices and toss to coat.
6. Place the apple slices in the air fryer basket. Ensure they are not overlapping; cook in batches if necessary.
7. Cook for 20 minutes, shaking the basket every 5 minutes.
8. After 20 minutes, increase the air fryer temperature to 165°C (330°F) and cook for another 2 minutes, shaking the basket every 30 seconds.
9. Remove the apples from the basket before they get too dark.
10. Spread the chips out onto paper towels to cool completely, at least 5 minutes.
11. Repeat with the remaining apple slices until they're all cooked.

Cayenne-spiced Roasted Pecans

Servings: 4
Cooking Time: 15 Minutes
Ingredients:

- 1/4 tsp chili powder
- Salt and pepper to taste
- 1/8 tsp cayenne pepper
- 1 tsp cumin powder
- 1 tsp cinnamon powder
- 1/8 tsp garlic powder
- 1/8 tsp onion powder
- 120g raw pecans
- 30g butter, melted
- 5g honey

Directions:

1. Preheat the air fryer to 150°C (300°F).
2. In a bowl, whisk together black pepper, chili powder, salt, cayenne pepper, cumin, garlic powder, cinnamon, and onion powder. Set the spice mixture aside.
3. Toss the raw pecans, melted butter, and honey in a medium bowl until the pecans are well coated.
4. Add the spice mixture to the pecans and toss them to ensure even distribution of the spices.
5. Pour the spiced pecans into the air fryer frying basket.

6. Toast the pecans for 3 minutes, stirring them once during this time.

7. After 3 minutes, stir the pecans again and toast for another 3 to 5 minutes until the nuts are crisp and have a roasted aroma.

8. Allow the roasted pecans to cool before serving.

Avocado Fries With Quick Salsa Fresca

Servings: 4
Cooking Time: 6 Minutes
Ingredients:

- 60 grams flour
- 2 teaspoons salt
- 2 eggs, lightly beaten
- 120 grams panko breadcrumbs
- 0.5 ml cayenne pepper
- 1.25 ml smoked paprika (optional)
- 2 large avocados, just ripe
- Vegetable oil, in a spray bottle
- Quick Salsa Fresca:
- 200 grams cherry tomatoes
- 1 tablespoon-sized chunk of shallot or red onion
- 10 ml fresh lime juice
- 5 ml chopped fresh cilantro or parsley
- Salt and freshly ground black pepper

Directions:

1. Set up a dredging station with three shallow dishes. Place the flour and salt in the first shallow dish. Place the eggs into the second dish. Combine the breadcrumbs, cayenne pepper, and paprika (if using) in the third dish.

2. Preheat the air fryer to 200°C (400°F).

3. Cut the avocado in half around the pit and separate the two sides. Slice the avocados into long strips while still in their skin. Run a spoon around the slices, separating them from the avocado skin. Try to keep the slices whole, but don't worry if they break – you can still coat and air-fry the pieces.

4. Coat the avocado slices by dredging them first in the flour, then the egg, and then the breadcrumbs, pressing the crumbs on gently with your hands. Set the coated avocado fries on a tray and spray them on all sides with vegetable oil.

5. Air-fry the avocado fries, one layer at a time, at 200°C (400°F) for 6 minutes, turning them over halfway

through the cooking time and spraying lightly again if necessary. When the fries are nicely browned on all sides, season with salt and remove.

6. While the avocado fries are air-frying, make the salsa fresca by combining all the salsa ingredients in a food processor. Pulse several times until the salsa is a chunky purée.

7. Serve the fries warm with the salsa on the side for dipping.

Basil Feta Crostini

Servings: 4
Cooking Time: 10 Minutes
Ingredients:

- 1 baguette, sliced
- 60 ml olive oil
- 2 garlic cloves, minced
- 115 grams feta cheese
- 2 tablespoons basil, minced

Directions:

1. Preheat the air fryer to 190°C (380°F).

2. In a bowl, combine the olive oil and minced garlic.

3. Brush the olive oil and garlic mixture over one side of each slice of bread.

4. Place the bread slices in a single layer in the air fryer basket and air fry for 5 minutes.

5. In a small bowl, mix together the feta cheese and minced basil.

6. Remove the toasted bread from the air fryer and spread a thin layer of the feta cheese and basil mixture over the top of each piece.

7. Serve and enjoy your Basil Feta Crostini.

Bagel Chips Recipes

Servings: 2
Cooking Time: 4 Minutes
Ingredients:

- Sweet:
- 1 large plain bagel
- 10 grams sugar
- 2.5 grams ground cinnamon
- Butter-flavored cooking spray
- Savory:
- 1 large plain bagel
- 5 grams Italian seasoning
- 2.5 grams garlic powder

- Oil for misting or cooking spray

Directions:

1. Preheat the air fryer to 200°C (390°F).

2. Cut the bagel into slices that are 0.6 cm (1/4 inch) thick or thinner.

3. Mix the seasonings together for either the sweet or savory version.

4. Spread out the bagel slices and mist them with oil or cooking spray. Sprinkle half of the seasonings on one side of the slices.

5. Turn the bagel slices over and repeat the process, coating the other side with oil or cooking spray and the remaining seasonings.

6. Place the coated bagel slices in the air fryer basket.

7. Cook the bagel slices in the air fryer for 2 minutes. Shake the basket or stir them a little, and then continue cooking for an additional 2 minutes or until they become toasty brown and crispy.

Cheddar Stuffed Pepper

Servings: 5
Cooking Time: 15 Minutes

Ingredients:

- 10 jalapeño peppers
- 170g ricotta cheese
- 60g grated cheddar cheese
- 30ml bread crumbs

Directions:

1. Preheat the air fryer to 170°C (340°F).

2. Cut the jalapeño peppers in half lengthwise and carefully remove the seeds and membrane. Set them aside.

3. Microwave the ricotta cheese in a small bowl for 15 seconds to soften it. Stir in the grated cheddar cheese to combine.

4. Stuff each jalapeño half with the cheese mixture.

5. Top the stuffed jalapeños with bread crumbs.

6. Place the stuffed jalapeños in the air fryer basket and lightly spray them with cooking oil.

7. Air fry the jalapeños for 5-6 minutes, or until they are heated through and the bread crumbs are golden.

8. Serve the Cheddar Stuffed Jalapeños warm.

Cajun-spiced Pickle Chips

Servings: 4
Cooking Time: 20 Minutes

Ingredients:

- 450g canned pickle slices
- 120g plain flour
- 30g cornmeal
- 3 tsp Cajun seasoning
- 1 tbsp dried parsley
- 1 egg, beaten
- 1/4 tsp hot sauce
- 120ml buttermilk
- 3 tbsp light mayonnaise
- 3 tbsp chopped chives
- 1/8 tsp garlic powder
- 1/8 tsp onion powder
- Salt and pepper to taste

Directions:

1. Preheat the air fryer to 175°C (350°F).

2. In a bowl, mix together the plain flour, cornmeal, Cajun seasoning, and dried parsley.

3. Place the beaten egg in a small bowl nearby.

4. One at a time, dip a pickle slice in the egg, ensuring it's coated, then roll it in the crumb mixture. Gently press the crumbs onto the pickle to make them stick.

5. Place the coated pickle chips in the greased frying basket of the air fryer.

6. Air fry the pickle chips for 7-9 minutes, flipping them once halfway through, or until they are golden and crispy.

7. In a separate bowl, whisk together the hot sauce, buttermilk, mayonnaise, chopped chives, garlic powder, onion powder, and season with salt and pepper to taste.

8. Serve the Cajun-spiced pickle chips with the dipping sauce.

Buffalo Chicken Wings

Servings: 6
Cooking Time: 60 Minutes

Ingredients:

- 900 grams chicken wings, split at the joint
- 15 ml butter, softened
- 120 ml buffalo wing sauce
- 5 ml salt
- 2.5 ml black pepper
- 2.5 ml red chili powder
- 2.5 ml garlic-ginger puree

Directions:

1. Preheat the air fryer to 200°C (400°F).

2. Sprinkle the chicken wings with salt, black pepper, red chili powder, garlic-ginger puree, and grated garlic. Toss to coat the wings evenly.

3. Place the seasoned chicken wings in the greased air fryer basket.

4. Air fry for 12 minutes, tossing the wings once during cooking to ensure even cooking.

5. While the wings are cooking, whisk together the softened butter and buffalo sauce in a large bowl.

6. After the initial 12 minutes of cooking, continue to air fry the wings for an additional 10 minutes, shaking the basket once during cooking.

7. · Once the chicken wings are cooked through and crispy, transfer them into the bowl with the buffalo sauce.

8. Toss the wings in the sauce to coat them evenly.

9. Serve the Buffalo Chicken Wings immediately.

Homemade Pretzel Bites

Servings: 8
Cooking Time: 6 Minutes
Ingredients:

- 1,125 ml (4¾ cups) filtered water, divided
- 15 ml (1 tablespoon) butter
- 1 package fast-rising yeast
- 2.5 ml (½ teaspoon) salt
- 550 ml (2⅓ cups) bread flour
- 30 ml (2 tablespoons) baking soda
- 2 egg whites
- 5 ml (1 teaspoon) kosher salt

Directions:

1. Preheat the air fryer to 188°C (370°F).

2. In a large microwave-safe bowl, add 180 ml (¾ cup) of the water. Heat for 40 seconds in the microwave. Remove and whisk in the butter; then mix in the yeast and salt. Let it sit for 5 minutes.

3. Using a stand mixer with a dough hook attachment, add the yeast liquid and mix in the bread flour 80 ml (⅓ cup) at a time until all the flour is added and a dough is formed.

4. Remove the bowl from the stand; then let the dough rise for 1 hour in a warm space, covered with a kitchen towel.

5. After the dough has doubled in size, remove it from the bowl and punch it down a few times on a lightly floured flat surface.

6. Divide the dough into 4 balls; then roll each ball out into a long, skinny, stick-like shape. Using a sharp knife, cut each dough stick into 6 pieces.

7. Repeat Step 6 for the remaining dough balls until you have about 24 bites formed.

8. Heat the remaining 945 ml (4 cups) of water over the stovetop in a medium pot with the baking soda stirred in.

9. Drop the pretzel bite dough into the hot water and let boil for 60 seconds, remove, and let them slightly cool.

10. Lightly brush the top of each bite with the egg whites, and then cover with a pinch of kosher salt.

11. Spray the air fryer basket with olive oil spray and place the pretzel bites on top. Cook for 6 to 8 minutes, or until lightly browned. Remove and keep warm.

12. Repeat until all pretzel bites are cooked.

13. Serve warm.

Chipotle Sunflower Seeds

Servings: 4
Cooking Time: 20 Minutes
Ingredients:

- 360g sunflower seeds
- 10ml olive oil
- 1.25g chipotle powder
- 1 garlic clove, minced
- 1.25g salt
- 5g granulated sugar

Directions:

1. Preheat the air fryer to 163°C (325°F).

2. In a bowl, mix the sunflower seeds, olive oil, chipotle powder, minced garlic, salt, and sugar until the seeds are well coated.

3. Place the mixture in the air fryer basket.

4. Air fry for 10 minutes, shaking the basket once during cooking to ensure even cooking.

5. Serve your Chipotle Sunflower Seeds chilled.

Buttery Spiced Pecans

Servings: 6
Cooking Time: 4 Minutes
Ingredients:

- 225 grams (½ pound) Pecan halves
- 30 grams Butter, melted
- 5 ml Mild paprika
- 2.5 ml Ground cumin
- Up to 2.5 ml Cayenne (adjust to taste)

- 2.5 ml Table salt

Directions:

1. Preheat the air fryer to 200°C (400°F).

2. Toss the pecans, melted butter, paprika, ground cumin, cayenne (adjust to taste), and salt in a bowl until the nuts are evenly coated.

3. When the air fryer reaches the desired temperature, pour the coated pecans into the basket, spreading them into as close to one layer as you can.

4. Air-fry the pecans for 4 minutes, tossing after every minute, and perhaps even more frequently for the last minute if the pecans are really browning. They should be warm, dark brown in spots, and very aromatic.

5. Pour the contents of the basket onto a lipped baking sheet and spread the nuts into one layer.

6. Allow the nuts to cool for at least 5 minutes before serving. The nuts can be stored at room temperature in a sealed container for up to 1 week.

Avocado Fries Recipes

Servings: 8
Cooking Time: 8 Minutes

Ingredients:

- 2 medium avocados, firm but ripe
- 1 large egg
- 2.5 ml garlic powder
- 1.25 ml cayenne pepper
- 1.25 ml salt
- 180 ml almond flour
- 120 grams finely grated Parmesan cheese
- 60 grams gluten-free breadcrumbs

Directions:

1. Preheat the air fryer to 190°C (370°F).

2. Rinse the outside of the avocados with water. Slice each avocado in half, slice each half in half again, and then slice each quarter in half once more to get 8 slices from each avocado. Remove the outer skin. Repeat for the other avocado. Set the avocado slices aside.

3. In a small bowl, whisk together the egg, garlic powder, cayenne pepper, and salt. Set aside.

4. In a separate bowl, place the almond flour.

5. In a third bowl, combine the Parmesan cheese and gluten-free breadcrumbs.

6. Carefully roll each avocado slice in the almond flour, then dip it in the egg wash, and coat it in the cheese and breadcrumb mixture. Repeat this process until all 16 fries are coated.

7. Liberally spray the air fryer basket with olive oil spray and place the avocado fries into the basket, leaving a little space around the sides between fries. Depending on the size of your air fryer, you may need to cook these in batches.

8. Cook the fries for 8 minutes or until the outer coating turns light brown.

9. Carefully remove the cooked fries, repeat with the remaining slices, and then serve them warm.

Buffalo Cauliflower

Servings: 6
Cooking Time: 12 Minutes

Ingredients:

- 1 large head of cauliflower, washed and cut into medium-size florets
- 60 ml all-purpose flour
- 60 ml melted butter
- 3 tablespoons hot sauce
- 2.5 ml garlic powder
- 120 ml blue cheese dip or ranch dressing (optional)

Directions:

1. Preheat the air fryer to 175°C (350°F).

2. Make sure the cauliflower florets are dry, and then coat them in flour.

3. Liberally spray the air fryer basket with an olive oil mist. Place the cauliflower into the basket, making sure not to stack them on top of each other. Depending on the size of your air fryer, you may need to do this in two batches.

4. Cook for 6 minutes, then shake the basket, and cook for an additional 6 minutes.

5. While the cauliflower is cooking, mix the melted butter, hot sauce, and garlic powder in a large bowl.

6. Carefully remove the cauliflower from the air fryer. Toss the cauliflower into the butter mixture to coat. Repeat Steps 2–4 for any leftover cauliflower.

7. Serve the Buffalo Cauliflower warm with the dip of your choice.

Cherry Chipotle Bbq Chicken Wings

Servings: 2
Cooking Time: 12 Minutes

Ingredients:

- 1 teaspoon smoked paprika
- 1/2 teaspoon dry mustard powder
- 1 teaspoon dried oregano
- 1 teaspoon dried thyme
- 1/2 teaspoon chili powder
- 1 teaspoon salt
- 900g chicken wings
- Vegetable oil or spray
- Salt and freshly ground black pepper
- 15-30ml chopped chipotle peppers in adobo sauce (adjust to your preferred level of spiciness)
- 80ml cherry preserves
- 60ml tomato ketchup

Directions:

1. Combine the first six ingredients in a large bowl.
2. Prepare the chicken wings by cutting off the wing tips and discarding them (or freezing them for chicken stock). Divide the drumettes from the wingettes by cutting through the joint. Place the chicken wing pieces in the bowl with the spice mix. Toss or shake well to coat.
3. Preheat the air fryer to 200°C (400°F).
4. Spray the wings lightly with vegetable oil or use cooking spray. Air-fry the wings in two batches for 10 minutes per batch, shaking the basket halfway through the cooking process. When both batches are done, toss all the wings back into the basket for another 2 minutes to heat through and finish cooking.
5. While the wings are air-frying, combine the chopped chipotle peppers, cherry preserves, and tomato ketchup in a bowl to make the cherry chipotle BBQ sauce.
6. Remove the wings from the air fryer, toss them in the cherry chipotle BBQ sauce, and serve with napkins!

Home-style Taro Chips

Servings: 2
Cooking Time: 20 Minutes

Ingredients:

- 15 ml (1 tbsp) olive oil
- 240 ml (1 cup) thinly sliced taro
- Salt to taste
- 120 ml (½ cup) hummus

Directions:

1. Preheat the air fryer to 163°C (325°F).
2. Place the sliced taro in the greased frying basket, spread the pieces out, and drizzle them with olive oil.
3. Air Fry for 10-12 minutes, shaking the basket twice during cooking.
4. Sprinkle the taro chips with salt to taste.
5. Serve the taro chips with hummus.

Honey-mustard Chicken Wings

Servings: 2
Cooking Time: 14 Minutes

Ingredients:

- 907 grams (2 pounds) chicken wings
- Salt and freshly ground black pepper
- 28 grams (2 tablespoons) butter
- 60 ml (1/4 cup) honey
- 60 ml (1/4 cup) spicy brown mustard
- Pinch of ground cayenne pepper
- 10 ml (2 teaspoons) Worcestershire sauce

Directions:

1. Prepare the chicken wings by cutting off the wing tips and discarding them (or freezing for chicken stock). Divide the drumettes from the wingettes by cutting through the joint. Place the chicken wing pieces in a large bowl.
2. Preheat the air fryer to 204°C (400°F).
3. Season the wings with salt and freshly ground black pepper.
4. Air-fry the wings in two batches for 10 minutes per batch, shaking the basket halfway through the cooking process.
5. While the wings are air-frying, combine the remaining ingredients (butter, honey, spicy brown mustard, ground cayenne pepper, and Worcestershire sauce) in a small saucepan over low heat. Stir and heat until the sauce is well combined and warmed.
6. When both batches of wings are done, toss all the wings with the honey-mustard sauce and place them back into the basket for another 4 minutes to heat through and finish cooking. Shake the basket periodically during this step to redistribute the wings for even cooking.
7. Remove the wings from the air fryer and serve.

Blooming Onion

Servings: 4
Cooking Time: 25 Minutes
Ingredients:

- 1 large Vidalia onion, peeled
- 2 eggs
- 120 ml milk
- 120 grams flour
- 5 ml salt
- 2.5 ml freshly ground black pepper
- 1.25 ml ground cayenne pepper
- 2.5 ml paprika
- 2.5 ml garlic powder
- Dipping Sauce:
- 120 ml mayonnaise
- 120 ml ketchup
- 5 ml Worcestershire sauce
- 2.5 ml ground cayenne pepper
- 2.5 ml paprika
- 2.5 ml onion powder

Directions:

1. Cut off the top inch of the onion, leaving the root end of the onion intact. Place the now flat, stem end of the onion down on a cutting board with the root end facing up. Make 16 slices around the onion, starting with your knife tip 3 cm away from the root so that you never slice through the root. Begin by making slices at 12, 3, 6, and 9 o'clock around the onion. Then make three slices down the onion in between each of the original four slices. Turn the onion over, gently separate the onion petals, and remove the loose pieces of onion in the center.

2. Combine the eggs and milk in a bowl. In a second bowl, combine the flour, salt, black pepper, cayenne pepper, paprika, and garlic powder.

3. Preheat the air fryer to 175°C (350°F).

4. Place the onion cut side up into a third empty bowl. Sprinkle the flour mixture all over the onion to cover it and get in between the onion petals. Turn the onion over to carefully shake off the excess flour, and then transfer the onion to the empty flour bowl, again cut side up.

5. Pour the egg mixture all over the onion to cover all the flour. Let it soak for a minute in the mixture. Carefully remove the onion, tipping it upside down to drain off any excess egg, and transfer it to the empty egg bowl, again cut side up.

6. Finally, sprinkle the flour mixture over the onion a second time, making sure the onion is well coated, and all the petals have the seasoned flour mixture on them. Carefully turn the onion over, shake off any excess flour, and transfer it to a plate or baking sheet. Spray the onion generously with vegetable oil.

7. Transfer the onion, cut side up, to the air fryer basket and air-fry for 25 minutes. The onion petals will open more fully as it cooks, so spray with more vegetable oil at least twice during the cooking time.

8. While the onion is cooking, make the dipping sauce by combining all the dip ingredients and mixing well.

9. Serve the Blooming Onion as soon as it comes out of the air fryer with dipping sauce on the side.

Herbed Cheese Brittle

Servings: 4
Cooking Time: 5 Minutes
Ingredients:

- 120g shredded Parmesan cheese
- 120g shredded white cheddar cheese
- 15ml fresh chopped rosemary
- 5ml garlic powder
- 1 large egg white

Directions:

1. Preheat the air fryer to 200°C (400°F).

2. In a large bowl, mix the cheeses, rosemary, and garlic powder. Mix in the egg white.

3. Pour the batter into a 17.78cm (7-inch) pan (or an air-fryer-compatible pan).

4. Place the pan in the air fryer basket and cook for 4 to 5 minutes, or until the cheese is melted and slightly browned.

5. Remove the pan from the air fryer, and let it cool for 2 minutes. Invert the pan before the cheese brittle completely cools but is semi-hardened to allow it to easily slide out of the pan.

6. Let the pan cool for another 5 minutes. Break into pieces and serve.

Bagel Chips

Servings: 3
Cooking Time: 8 Minutes
Ingredients:

- 2 Plain, whole-wheat, pumpernickel, or salt bagels
- Vegetable oil or olive oil spray

Directions:

1. Preheat the air fryer to 200°C (400°F).
2. Lay a bagel flat on a cutting board and slice it across its circular surface into strips that are approximately 0.3 cm (1/8 inch) wide. Place these strips in a bowl, and continue to make more bagel strips as needed. Some strips may be cut through the hole and end up as two smaller strips, and others may be shorter due to their location on the bagel.
3. Lightly coat the bagel strips with vegetable or olive oil spray. Toss them well to ensure even coating, and repeat the oil spray as needed until every piece is evenly coated but not greasy.
4. Pour the coated bagel strips into the air fryer basket.
5. Air-fry the bagel strips, tossing the basket and rearranging the strips three or four times, for 8 minutes or until they become lightly browned, with a slight blackening at the edges. Be vigilant as the chips can burn quickly, and do not leave the machine unattended.
6. Once the chips are ready, transfer them to a wire rack to cool. Allow them to cool for a few minutes before serving them warm. Alternatively, you can let them cool to room temperature, which takes about 1 hour.

Buffalo Bites

Servings: 16
Cooking Time: 12 Minutes
Ingredients:

- 450 grams ground chicken
- 4 tablespoons buffalo wing sauce
- 56 grams Gruyère cheese, cut into 16 cubes
- 15 ml maple syrup

Directions:

1. Mix 2 tablespoons of buffalo wing sauce into the ground chicken.
2. Shape the chicken mixture into a log and divide it into 16 equal portions.
3. With slightly damp hands, mold each portion of chicken around a cube of Gruyère cheese and shape it into a firm ball.
4. When you have shaped 8 meatballs, place them in the air fryer basket.
5. Cook at 200°C (390°F) for approximately 5 minutes. Shake the basket, reduce the temperature to 180°C (360°F), and cook for an additional 5 minutes.
6. While the first batch is cooking, shape the remaining chicken and cheese into 8 more meatballs.
7. Repeat step 5 to cook the second batch of meatballs.
8. In a medium bowl, mix the remaining 2 tablespoons of buffalo wing sauce with the maple syrup. Add all the cooked meatballs and toss to coat.
9. Place the meatballs back into the air fryer basket and cook at 200°C (390°F) for 2 minutes to set the glaze.
10. Skewer each meatball with a toothpick and serve.

Avocado Balls

Servings: 6
Cooking Time: 25 Minutes + Freezing Time
Ingredients:

- 2 avocados, peeled
- 15 ml minced cilantro
- 15 ml lime juice
- 2.5 ml salt
- 1 egg, beaten
- 15 ml milk
- 60 ml almond flour
- 120 ml ground almonds

Directions:

1. Preheat the air fryer to 200°C (400°F).
2. In a bowl, mash the peeled avocados with minced cilantro, lime juice, and salt.
3. Line a baking sheet with parchment paper and shape the avocado mixture into 12 balls. You can use an ice cream scoop or a 30 ml (1/8-cup) measure to portion them. Place the formed balls on the baking sheet and freeze for 2 hours.
4. In a shallow bowl, beat the egg and mix in the milk.
5. On a plate, combine the almond flour and ground almonds.
6. Dip each frozen avocado ball into the egg mixture, ensuring it's coated, and then roll it in the almond mixture, coating it evenly.
7. Place half of the avocado balls in the freezer while you cook the first batch.

8. Arrange the remaining 6 avocado balls in the air fryer basket, mist them with olive oil, and Air Fry for 4-5 minutes or until they turn golden.

9. Repeat the cooking process with the second batch.

10. Serve and enjoy your Avocado Balls!

Asian-style Shrimp Toast

Servings: 4
Cooking Time: 25 Minutes
Ingredients:

- 8 large raw shrimp, chopped
- 1 egg white
- 2 garlic cloves, minced
- 1 red chili, minced
- 1 celery stalk, minced
- 2 tablespoons cornstarch
- 1/4 teaspoon Chinese five-spice powder
- 3 slices of firm bread

Directions:

1. Preheat the air fryer to 180°C (350°F).

2. In a bowl, combine the chopped shrimp, egg white, minced garlic, minced red chili, minced celery, cornstarch, and Chinese five-spice powder.

3. Place 1/3 of the shrimp mixture on a slice of bread, spreading it evenly to the edges. Then, cut the bread into 4 strips.

4. Lay the prepared strips in the air fryer basket in a single layer.

5. Air Fry for 3-6 minutes or until the shrimp toast strips are golden and crispy. Repeat this process until all the strips are cooked.

6. Serve the Asian-Style Shrimp Toast hot.

Mozzarella Stuffed Mushrooms

Servings: 4
Cooking Time: 30 Minutes
Ingredients:

- 16 button mushrooms
- 80 ml salsa
- 3 garlic cloves, minced
- 1 onion, finely chopped
- 1 jalapeño pepper, minced
- 1/8 tsp cayenne pepper
- 45 grams shredded mozzarella
- 10 ml olive oil

- Instructions:
- Preheat your air fryer to 175°C (350°F).
- Begin by removing the stems from the mushrooms and finely chopping them. Set the mushroom caps aside.
- In a bowl, combine the salsa, minced garlic, finely chopped onion, minced jalapeño pepper, cayenne pepper, and shredded mozzarella cheese. Add the chopped mushroom stems to this mixture and mix well.
- Fill each mushroom cap generously with the mixture, allowing it to slightly overflow from the top of the caps.
- Drizzle olive oil over the stuffed mushroom caps.
- Place the stuffed mushroom caps in the air fryer and bake for 8-12 minutes. The filling should become hot, and the mushrooms should turn soft.
- Serve the Jalapeño & Mozzarella Stuffed Mushrooms while they're still warm.

Vegan Avocado Fries

Servings: 4
Cooking Time: 10 Minutes
Ingredients:

- 60 ml almond or coconut milk
- 15 ml lime juice
- 0.5 ml hot sauce
- 30 ml flour
- 90 grams panko breadcrumbs
- 30 grams cornmeal
- 1/4 teaspoon salt
- 1 large avocado
- Oil for misting or cooking spray

Directions:

1. In a small bowl, whisk together the almond or coconut milk, lime juice, and hot sauce.

2. Place the flour on a sheet of parchment paper.

3. Mix the panko breadcrumbs, cornmeal, and salt together and place them on another sheet of parchment paper.

4. Split the avocado in half and remove the pit. Peel the avocado halves or use a spoon to lift the avocado halves out of the skin.

5. Cut the avocado lengthwise into 1.25 cm (1/2-inch) slices. Dip each avocado slice in flour, then in the milk mixture, and finally roll it in the panko mixture to coat it evenly.

6. Mist the coated avocado slices with oil or use a cooking spray.

7. Cook the avocado fries in the air fryer at 200°C (390°F) for 10 minutes or until the crust is brown and crispy.

Black-olive Poppers

Servings: 5
Cooking Time: 20 Minutes
Ingredients:

- 5 jalapeño peppers, cut lengthwise, seeded
- 60 ml cream cheese, softened
- 60 ml grated cheddar
- 15 ml chopped black olives
- 15 ml chopped green olives
- 5 ml dried oregano
- 15 ml mayonnaise
- 15 ml Parmesan cheese
- 15 ml dried parsley

Directions:

1. Preheat the air fryer to 180°C (350°F).
2. Mix all ingredients, except for the jalapeño peppers, in a bowl.
3. Add the prepared mixture into each jalapeño half.
4. Lay the stuffed peppers in the air fryer basket.
5. Bake for 8 minutes in the preheated air fryer.
6. Transfer the jalapeño poppers to a serving plate.
7. Serve them right away and sprinkle with dried parsley.

Brie-currant & Bacon Spread

Servings: 6
Cooking Time: 30 Minutes
Ingredients:

- 115 grams cream cheese, softened
- 45 ml mayonnaise
- 225 grams diced Brie cheese
- 2.5 ml dried thyme
- 115 grams cooked bacon, crumbled
- 80 ml dried currants

Directions:

1. Preheat the air fryer to 175°C (350°F).
2. Beat the cream cheese with the mayonnaise until well blended.
3. Stir in the Brie, dried thyme, crumbled bacon, and dried currants.
4. Pour the dip mixture into a 15 cm (6-inch) round pan.

5. Place the pan in the air fryer and air fry for 10-12 minutes, stirring once during cooking, until the dip is melting and bubbling.
6. Serve the Brie-Currant & Bacon Spread warm.

Baba Ghanouj

Servings: 2
Cooking Time: 40 Minutes
Ingredients:

- 2 small (340 grams each) purple Italian eggplants
- 60 ml Olive oil
- 60 ml Tahini
- 1/2 teaspoon Ground black pepper
- 1/4 teaspoon Onion powder
- 1/4 teaspoon Mild smoked paprika (optional)
- Up to 1 teaspoon Table salt

Directions:

1. Preheat the air fryer to 200°C (400°F).
2. Prick the eggplants on all sides with a fork. Once the air fryer has reached the desired temperature, place the eggplants in the basket in one layer. Air-fry them undisturbed for 40 minutes, or until they become blackened and soft.
3. Remove the basket from the air fryer. Allow the eggplants to cool in the basket for 20 minutes.
4. Use a nonstick-safe spatula, and perhaps a flatware tablespoon for balance, to gently transfer the eggplants to a bowl. The juices will run out, so make sure the bowl is close to the basket. Split the eggplants open.
5. Scrape the soft insides of half an eggplant into a food processor. Repeat this process with the remaining piece(s). Add any juices from the bowl to the eggplant in the food processor, but discard the skins and stems.
6. Add the olive oil, tahini, ground black pepper, onion powder, and smoked paprika (if using). Start by adding about half of the salt. Then, cover and process until smooth, stopping the machine at least once to scrape down the inside of the canister. Taste the spread for salt and add more as needed.
7. Scrape the baba ghanouj into a bowl and serve it warm, or set it aside at room temperature for up to 2 hours. You can also cover and store it in the refrigerator for up to 4 days.

Arancini With Sun-dried Tomatoes And Mozzarella

Servings: 6
Cooking Time: 15 Minutes
Ingredients:

- 15ml olive oil
- ½ small onion, finely chopped
- 190g Arborio rice
- 60ml white wine or dry vermouth
- 240ml vegetable or chicken stock
- 360ml water
- 1 teaspoon salt
- freshly ground black pepper
- 80g grated Parmigiano-Reggiano cheese
- 57-85g mozzarella cheese
- 2 eggs, lightly beaten
- 60g chopped oil-packed sun-dried tomatoes
- 180g Italian seasoned breadcrumbs, divided
- olive oil
- marinara sauce, for serving

Directions:

1. Cook the Arborio Rice:

2. Stovetop Method: Preheat a medium saucepan over medium heat. Add the olive oil and sauté the onion until it starts to become tender – about 5 minutes. Add the rice and stir well to coat all the grains of rice. Add the white wine or vermouth. Let this simmer and get absorbed by the rice. Then add the stock and water, cover, reduce the heat to low and simmer for 20 minutes.

3. Pressure-Cooker Method: Preheat the pressure cooker using the BROWN setting. Add the oil and cook the onion for a few minutes. Add the rice, wine, stock, water, salt and freshly ground black pepper, give everything one good stir and lock the lid in place. Pressure cook on HIGH for 7 minutes. Reduce the pressure with the QUICK-RELEASE method and carefully remove the lid.

4. Taste the rice to make sure it is tender. Season with salt and freshly ground black pepper and stir in the grated Parmigiano-Reggiano cheese. Spread the rice out onto a baking sheet to cool.

5. While the rice is cooling, cut the mozzarella into 2cm cubes.

6. Once the rice has cooled, combine the rice with the eggs, sun-dried tomatoes and 120g of the breadcrumbs. Place the remaining breadcrumbs in a shallow dish. Shape the rice mixture into 12 balls. Press a hole in the rice ball with your finger and push one or two cubes of mozzarella cheese into the hole. Mold the rice back into a ball, enclosing the cheese. Roll the finished rice balls in the breadcrumbs and place them on a baking sheet while you make the remaining rice balls. Spray or brush the rice balls with olive oil.

7. Preheat the air fryer to 190°C (380°F).

8. Cook 6 arancini at a time. Air-fry for 10 minutes. Gently turn the arancini over, brush or spray with oil again and air-fry for another 5 minutes. Serve warm with the marinara sauce.

Blistered Shishito Peppers

Servings: 3
Cooking Time: 5 Minutes
Ingredients:

- 170 grams (about 18) Shishito peppers
- Vegetable oil spray
- Coarse sea salt or kosher salt, for garnishing
- Lemon wedges

Directions:

1. Preheat the air fryer to 200°C (400°F).

2. Place the Shishito peppers in a bowl and lightly coat them with vegetable oil spray. Toss gently, spray again, and toss until the peppers are glistening but not drenched.

3. Pour the peppers into the air fryer basket, spreading them into as close to one layer as you can.

4. Air-fry the peppers for 5 minutes, tossing and rearranging the peppers at the 2- and 4-minute marks, until the peppers are blistered and even blackened in spots.

5. Transfer the blistered peppers to a bowl, add salt to taste, and toss gently.

6. Serve the peppers with lemon wedges to squeeze over them.

Garlic-herb Pita Chips

Servings: 4
Cooking Time: 6 Minutes
Ingredients:

- 1.25ml dried basil
- 1.25ml marjoram
- 1.25ml ground oregano
- 1.25ml garlic powder
- 1.25ml ground thyme
- 1.25ml salt
- 2 whole 15cm (6-inch) pitas, whole grain or white
- Oil for misting or cooking spray

Directions:

1. Mix all the seasonings together.
2. Cut each pita half into 4 wedges. Break apart the wedges at the fold.
3. Mist one side of the pita wedges with oil. Sprinkle them with half of the seasoning mix.
4. Turn the pita wedges over, mist the other side with oil, and sprinkle with the remaining seasonings.
5. Place the pita wedges in the air fryer basket and cook at 165°C (330°F) for 2 minutes.
6. Shake the basket and cook for 2 minutes longer. Shake again, and if needed, cook for 2 more minutes until they become crisp. Watch carefully because at this point, they will cook very quickly.

Beef & Lamb And Pork Recipes

Italian Meatballs

Servings: 12
Cooking Time:xx
Ingredients:

- 2 tbsp olive oil
- 2 tbsp minced shallot
- 3 cloves garlic minced
- 100g panko crumbs
- 35g chopped parsley
- 1 tbsp chopped rosemary
- 60ml milk
- 400g minced pork
- 250g turkey sausage
- 1 egg beaten
- 1 tbsp dijon mustard
- 1 tbsp finely chopped thyme

Directions:

1. Preheat air fryer to 200°C
2. Heat oil in a pan and cook the garlic and shallot over a medium heat for 1-2 minutes
3. Mix the panko and milk in a bowl and allow to stand for 5 minutes
4. Add all the ingredients to the panko mix and combine well
5. Shape into 1 ½ inch meatballs and cook for 12 minutes

Pulled Pork, Bacon, And Cheese Sliders

Servings:2
Cooking Time:30 Minutes
Ingredients:

- 2 x 50 g / 3.5 oz pork steaks
- 1 tsp salt
- 1 tsp black pepper
- 4 slices bacon strips, chopped into small pieces
- 1 tbsp soy sauce
- 1 tbsp BBQ sauce
- 100 g / 7 oz cheddar cheese, grated
- 2 bread buns

Directions:

1. Preheat the air fryer to 200 °C / 400 °F and line the bottom of the basket with parchment paper.

2. Place the pork steaks on a clean surface and season with salt and black pepper. Move the pork steak in the prepared air fryer basket and cook for 15 minutes.

3. Remove the steak from the air fryer and shred using two forks. Mix with the chopped bacon in a heatproof bowl and place the bowl in the air fryer. Cook for 10 minutes.

4. Remove the bowl from the air fryer and stir in the soy sauce and BBQ sauce. Return the bowl to the air fryer basket and continue cooking for a further 5 minutes.

5. Meanwhile, spread the cheese across one half of the bread buns. Top with the cooked pulled pork and an extra squirt of BBQ sauce.

Roast Beef

Servings: 2
Cooking Time:xx
Ingredients:
- 400g beef fillet
- 1 tbsp olive oil
- 1 tsp salt
- 1 tsp rosemary

Directions:
1. Preheat the air fryer to 180°C
2. Mix salt, rosemary and oil on a plate
3. Coat the beef with the mix
4. Place the beef in the air fryer and cook for 45 minutes turning halfway

Salt And Pepper Belly Pork

Servings: 4
Cooking Time:xx
Ingredients:
- 500g belly pork
- 1 tsp pepper
- ½ tsp salt

Directions:
1. Cut the pork into bite size pieces and season with salt and pepper
2. Heat the air fryer to 200°C
3. Place in the air fryer and cook for 15 minutes until crisp

Beef Wellington

Servings: 4
Cooking Time:xx
Ingredients:
- 300g chicken liver pate
- 500g shortcrust pastry
- 600g beef fillet
- 1 egg beaten
- Salt and pepper

Directions:
1. Remove all the visible fat from the beef season with salt and pepper. Wrap in cling film and place in the fridge for 1 hour
2. Roll out the pastry, brush the edges with egg
3. Spread the pate over the pastry. Remove the clingfilm from the beef and place in the center of the pastry
4. Seal the pastry around the meat
5. Place in the air fryer and cook at 160°C for 35 minutes

Homemade Crispy Pepperoni Pizza

Servings:4
Cooking Time:10 Minutes
Ingredients:
- For the pizza dough:
- 500 g / 17.6 oz plain flour
- 1 tsp salt
- 1 tsp dry non-fast-acting yeast
- 400 ml warm water
- For the toppings:
- 100 g / 3.5 oz tomato sauce
- 100 g / 3.5 oz mozzarella cheese, grated
- 8 slices pepperoni

Directions:
1. To make the pizza dough, place the plain flour, salt, and dry yeast in a large mixing bowl. Pour in the warm water bit by bit until it forms a tacky dough.

2. Lightly dust a clean kitchen top surface with plain flour and roll the dough out until it is around ½ an inch thick.

3. Preheat your air fryer to 150 °C / 300 °F and line the bottom of the basket with parchment paper.

4. Spread the tomato sauce evenly across the dough and top with grated mozzarella cheese. Top with the

pepperoni slices and carefully transfer the pizza into the lined air fryer basket.

5. Cook the pizza until the crust is golden and crispy, and the mozzarella cheese has melted.

6. Enjoy the pizza while still hot with a side salad and some potato wedges.

Mustard Glazed Pork

Servings: 4
Cooking Time:xx
Ingredients:

- 500g pork tenderloin
- 1 tbsp minced garlic
- ¼ tsp salt
- ⅛ tsp cracked black pepper
- 75g yellow mustard
- 3 tbsp brown sugar
- 1 tsp Italian seasoning
- 1 tsp rosemary

Directions:

1. Cut slits into the pork place the minced garlic into the slits, season with the salt and pepper

2. Add the remaining ingredients to a bowl and whisk to combine

3. Rub the mix over the pork and allow to marinate for 2 hours

4. Place in the air fryer and cook at 200ºC for 20 minutes

Cheeseburger Egg Rolls

Servings: 4
Cooking Time:xx
Ingredients:

- 400g minced beef
- ¼ tsp garlic powder
- ¼ tsp onion powder
- 1 chopped red pepper
- 1 chopped onion
- 6 dill pickles, chopped
- Salt and pepper
- 3 tbsp grated cheese
- 3 tbsp cream cheese
- 2 tbsp ketchup
- 1 tbsp mustard
- 6 large egg roll wrappers

Directions:

1. Cook the pepper, onion and minced beef in a pan for about 5 minutes

2. Remove from heat and stir in cheese, cream cheese, ketchup and mustard

3. Put the mix into a bowl and stir in the pickles

4. Place ⅙ of the mix in the centre of each wrap, moisten the edges with water roll up the wrap around the mixture and seal

5. Set your fryer to 200ºC and cook for about 7 minutes

6. Turn the sandwich over and cook for another 3 minutes

7. Turn the sandwich out and serve whilst hot

8. Repeat with the other remaining sandwich

Cheese & Ham Sliders

Servings: 4
Cooking Time:xx
Ingredients:

- 8 slider bread rolls, cut in half
- 16 slices of sweet ham
- 16 slices of Swiss cheese
- 5 tbsp mayonnaise
- 1/2 tsp paprika
- 1 tsp onion powder
- 1 tsp dill

Directions:

1. Place 2 slices of ham into each bread roll and 2 slices of cheese

2. Take a bowl and combine the mayonnaise with the onion powder, dill and paprika

3. Add half a tablespoon of the sauce on top of each piece of cheese

4. Place the top on the bread slider

5. Cook at 220ºC for 5 minutes

Buttermilk Pork Chops

Servings: 4
Cooking Time:xx
Ingredients:

- 4 pork chops
- 3 tbsp buttermilk
- 75g flour
- Cooking oil spray
- 1 packet of pork rub
- Salt and pepper to taste

Directions:

1. Rub the chops with the pork rub
2. Place the pork chops in a bowl and drizzle with buttermilk
3. Coat the chops with flour
4. Place in the air fryer and cook at 190ºC for 15 minutes turning halfway

Beef Stuffed Peppers

Servings: 4
Cooking Time:xx
Ingredients:

- 4 bell peppers
- ½ chopped onion
- 1 minced garlic clove
- 500g minced beef
- 5 tbsp tomato sauce
- 100g grated cheese
- 2 tsp Worcestershire sauce
- 1 tsp garlic powder
- A pinch of black pepper
- ½ tsp chilli powder
- 1 tsp dried basil
- 75g cooked rice

Directions:

1. Cook the onions, minced beef, garlic and all the seasonings until the meat is browned
2. Remove from the heat and add Worcestershire sauce, rice, ½ the cheese and ⅔ of the tomato sauce mix well
3. Cut the tops off the peppers and remove the seeds
4. Stuff the peppers with the mixture and place in the air fryer
5. Cook at 200ºC for about 11 minutes
6. When there are 3 minutes remaining top the peppers with the rest of the tomato sauce and cheese

Pork Chops With Honey

Servings: 6
Cooking Time:xx
Ingredients:

- 2 ⅔ tbsp honey
- 100g ketchup
- 6 pork chops
- 2 cloves of garlic
- 2 slices mozzarella cheese

Directions:

1. Preheat air fryer to 200ºC
2. Mix all the ingredients together in a bowl
3. Add the pork chops, allow to marinate for at least 1 hour
4. Place in the air fryer and cook for about 12 minutes turning halfway

Char Siu Buffalo

Servings: 2
Cooking Time:xx
Ingredients:

- 1 kg beef, cut into strips
- 4 tbsp honey
- 2 tbsp sugar
- 2 tbsp char siu sauce
- 2 tbsp oyster sauce
- 2 tbsp soy sauce
- 2 tbsp olive oil
- 2 tsp minced garlic
- ¼ tsp bi carbonate of soda

Directions:

1. Place all the ingredients in a bowl, mix well and marinate over night
2. Line the air fryer with foil, add the beef, keep the marinade to one side
3. Cook at 200ºC for 10 minutes
4. Brush the pork with the sauce and cook for another 20 minutes at 160ºC
5. Remove the meat and set aside
6. Strain the marinade into a saucepan, heat until it thickens
7. Drizzle over the pork and serve with rice

Tahini Beef Bites

Servings: 2
Cooking Time:xx
Ingredients:

- 500g sirloin steak, cut into cubes
- 2 tbsp Za'atar seasoning
- 1 tsp olive oil
- 25g Tahini
- 25g warm water
- 1 tbsp lemon juice
- 1 clove of garlic

- Salt to taste

Directions:

1. Preheat the air fryer to 250ºC

2. Take a bowl and combine the oil with the steak, salt, and Za'atar seasoning

3. Place in the air fryer and cook for 10 minutes, turning halfway through

4. Take a bowl and combine the water, garlic, lemon juice, salt, and tahini, or use a food processor if you have one

5. Pour the sauce over the bites and serve

Steak And Mushrooms

Servings: 4

Cooking Time:xx

Ingredients:

- 500g cubed sirloin steak
- 300g button mushrooms
- 3 tbsp Worcestershire sauce
- 1 tbsp olive oil
- 1 tsp parsley flakes
- 1 tsp paprika
- 1 tsp crushed chilli flakes

Directions:

1. Combine all ingredients in a bowl, cover and chill for at least 4 hours

2. Preheat air fryer to 200ºC

3. Drain and discard the marinade from the steak

4. Place the steak and mushrooms in the air fryer and cook for 5 minutes

5. Toss and cook for a further 5 minutes

Breaded Pork Chops

Servings: 6

Cooking Time:xx

Ingredients:

- 6 boneless pork chops
- 1 beaten egg
- 100g panko crumbs
- 75g crushed cornflakes
- 2 tbsp parmesan
- 1 ¼ tsp paprika
- ½ tsp garlic powder
- ½ tsp onion powder
- ¼ tsp chilli powder

- Salt and pepper to taste

Directions:

1. Heat the air fryer to 200ºC

2. Season the pork chops with salt

3. Mix the panko, cornflakes, salt, parmesan, garlic powder, onion powder, paprika, chilli powder and pepper in a bowl

4. Beat the egg in another bowl

5. Dip the pork in the egg and then coat with panko mix

6. Place in the air fryer and cook for about 12 minutes turning halfway

Roast Pork

Servings: 4

Cooking Time:xx

Ingredients:

- 500g pork joint
- 1 tbsp olive oil
- 1 tsp salt

Directions:

1. Preheat air fryer to 180ºC

2. Score the pork skin with a knife

3. Drizzle the pork with oil and rub it into the skin, sprinkle with salt

4. Place in the air fryer and cook for about 50 minutes

Southern Style Pork Chops

Servings: 4

Cooking Time:xx

Ingredients:

- 4 pork chops
- 3 tbsp buttermilk
- 100g flour
- Salt and pepper to taste
- Pork rub to taste

Directions:

1. Season the pork with pork rub

2. Drizzle with buttermilk

3. Coat in flour until fully covered

4. Place the pork chops in the air fryer, cook at 170ºC for 15 minutes

5. Turnover and cook for a further 10 minutes

Mustard Pork Tenderloin

Servings: 2
Cooking Time:xx
Ingredients:
- 1 pork tenderloin
- 3 tbsp soy sauce
- 2 minced garlic cloves
- 3 tbsp olive oil
- 2 tbsp brown sugar
- 1 tbsp dijon mustard
- Salt and pepper for seasoning

Directions:
1. Take a bowl and combine the ingredients, except for the pork
2. Pour the mixture into a ziplock bag and then add the pork
3. Close the top and make sure the pork is well covered
4. Place in the refrigerator for 30minutes
5. Preheat your air fryer to 260ºC
6. Remove the pork from the bag and place in the fryer
7. Cook for 25 minutes, turning halfway
8. Remove and rest for 5 minutes before slicing into pieces

Pizza Dogs

Servings: 2
Cooking Time:xx
Ingredients:
- 2 pork hot dogs
- 4 pepperoni slices, halved
- 150g pizza sauce
- 2 hotdog buns
- 75g grated cheese
- 2 tsp sliced olives

Directions:
1. Preheat air fryer to 190ºC
2. Place 4 slits down each hotdog, place in the air fryer and cook for 3 minutes
3. Place a piece of pepperoni into each slit, add pizza sauce to hot dog buns
4. Place hotdogs in the buns and top with cheese and olives
5. Cook in the air fryer for about 2 minutes

Meatloaf

Servings: 2
Cooking Time:xx
Ingredients:
- 500g minced pork
- 1 egg
- 3 tbsp breadcrumbs
- 2 mushrooms thickly sliced
- 1 tbsp olive oil
- 1 chopped onion
- 1 tbsp chopped thyme
- 1 tsp salt
- Ground black pepper

Directions:
1. Preheat air fryer to 200ºC
2. Combine all the ingredients in a bowl
3. Put the mix into a pan and press down firmly, coat with olive oil
4. Place pan in the air fryer and cook for 25 minutes

Old Fashioned Steak

Servings: 4
Cooking Time:xx
Ingredients:
- 4 medium steaks
- 100g flour
- ½ tsp garlic powder
- Salt and pepper
- 1 egg
- 4 slices bacon
- 350ml milk

Directions:
1. Beat the egg
2. Mix the flour with garlic powder, salt and pepper
3. Dip the steak into the egg then cover in the flour mix
4. Place in the air fryer and cook at 170ºC for 7 minutes, turnover and cook for another 10 minutes until golden brown
5. Whilst the steak is cooking, place the bacon in a frying pan, stir in the flour. Add milk to the bacon and stir until there are no lumps in the flour
6. Season with salt and pepper Cook for 2 minutes until thickened season with salt and pepper

Lamb Burgers

Servings: 4
Cooking Time:xx
Ingredients:
- 600g minced lamb
- 2 tsp garlic puree
- 1 tsp harissa paste
- 2 tbsp Moroccan spice
- Salt and pepper

Directions:
1. Place all the ingredients in a bowl and mix well
2. Form into patties
3. Place in the air fryer and cook at 180ºC for 18 minutes

Japanese Pork Chops

Servings: 4
Cooking Time:xx
Ingredients:
- 6 boneless pork chops
- 30g flour
- 2 beaten eggs
- 2 tbsp sweet chilli sauce
- 500g cup seasoned breadcrumbs
- ⅛ tsp salt
- ⅛ tsp pepper
- Tonkatsu sauce to taste

Directions:
1. Place the flour, breadcrumbs and eggs in 3 separate bowls
2. Sprinkle both sides of the pork with salt and pepper
3. Coat the pork in flour, egg and then breadcrumbs
4. Place in the air fryer and cook at 180ºC for 8 minutes, turn then cook for a further 5 minutes
5. Serve with sauces on the side

Fillet Mignon Wrapped In Bacon

Servings: 2
Cooking Time:xx
Ingredients:
- 1 kg filet mignon
- 500g bacon slices
- Olive oil

Directions:
1. Wrap the fillets in bacon

2. Season with salt and pepper and brush with olive oil
3. Place in the air fryer cook at 200ºC for 9 minutes turning halfway through

Lamb Calzone

Servings: 2
Cooking Time:xx
Ingredients:
- 1 tsp olive oil
- 1 chopped onion
- 100g baby spinach leaves
- 400g minced pork
- 250g whole wheat pizza dough
- 300g grated cheese

Directions:
1. Heat the olive oil in a pan, add the onion and cook for about 2 minutes
2. Add the spinach and cook for a further 1 ½ minutes
3. Stir in marinara sauce and the minced pork
4. Divide the dough into four and roll out into circles
5. Add ¼ of filling to each piece of dough
6. Sprinkle with cheese and fold the dough over to create half moons, crimp edges to seal
7. Spray with cooking spray, place in the air fryer and cook at 160ºC for 12 minutes turning after 8 minutes

Pork With Chinese 5 Spice

Servings: 4
Cooking Time:xx
Ingredients:
- 2 pork rounds cut into chunks
- 2 large eggs
- 1 tsp sesame oil
- 200g cornstarch
- 1/4 tsp salt
- ½ tsp pepper
- 3 tbsp canola oil
- 1 tsp Chinese 5 spice

Directions:
1. In a bowl mix the corn starch, salt, pepper and 5 spice
2. Mix the eggs and sesame oil in another bowl
3. Dip the pork into the egg and then cover in the corn starch mix
4. Place in the air fryer and cook at 170ºC for 11-12 minutes, shaking halfway through
5. Serve with sweet and sour sauce

Asparagus & Steak Parcels

Servings: 4
Cooking Time:xx
Ingredients:

* 500g flank steak, cut into 6 equal pieces
* 75ml Tamari sauce
* 2 crushed garlic cloves
* 250g trimmed asparagus
* 3 large bell peppers, thinly sliced
* 2 tbsp butter
* Salt and pepper to taste

Directions:

1. Season the steak to your liking
2. Place the meat in a zip top bag and add the Tamari and garlic, sealing the bag closed
3. Make sure the steaks are fully coated in the sauce and leave them in the fright at least 1 hour, but preferably overnight
4. Remove the steaks from the bag and throw the marinade away
5. Place the peppers and sliced asparagus in the centre of each steak piece
6. Roll the steak up and secure in place with a tooth pick
7. Preheat your air fryer to 250ºC
8. Transfer the meat parcels to the air fryer and cook for 5 minutes
9. Allow to rest before serving
10. Melt the butter in a saucepan, over a medium heat, adding the juices from the air fryer
11. Combine well and keep cooking until thickened
12. Pour the sauce over the steak parcels and season to your liking

Cheesy Meatballs

Servings: 2
Cooking Time:xx
Ingredients:

* 500g ground beef
* 1 can of chopped green chillis
* 1 egg white
* 1 tbsp water
* 2 tbsp taco seasoning
* 16 pieces of pepper jack cheese, cut into cubes
* 300g nacho cheese tortilla chips, crushed
* 6 tbsp taco sauce
* 3 tbsp honey

Directions:

1. Take a large bowl and combine the beef with the green collie sand taco seasoning
2. Use your hands to create meatballs - you should get around 15 balls in total
3. Place a cube of cheese in the middle of each meatball, forming the ball around it once more
4. Take a small bowl and beat the egg white
5. Take a large bowl and add the crushed chips
6. Dip every meatball into the egg white and then the crushed chips
7. Place the balls into the air fryer and cook at 260ºC for 14 minutes, turning halfway
8. Take a microwave-safe bowl and combine the honey and taco sauce
9. Place in the microwave for 30 seconds and serve the sauce warm with the meatballs

Traditional Pork Chops

Servings: 8
Cooking Time:xx
Ingredients:

* 8 pork chops
* 1 egg
* 100ml milk
* 300g bread crumbs
* 1 packet of dry ranch seasoning mix
* Salt and pepper to taste

Directions:

1. Preheat air fryer to 170ºC
2. Beat the egg in a bowl, add the milk season with salt and pepper
3. In another bowl mix the bread crumbs and ranch dressing mix
4. Dip the pork into the egg then cover with breadcrumbs
5. Place in the air fryer and cook for 12 minutes turning half way

Beef Satay

Servings: 2
Cooking Time:xx
Ingredients:
- 400g steak strips
- 2 tbsp oil
- 1 tbsp fish sauce
- 1 tsp sriracha sauce
- 200g sliced coriander (fresh)
- 1 tsp ground coriander
- 1 tbsp soy
- 1 tbsp minced ginger
- 1 tbsp minced garlic
- 1 tbsp sugar
- 25g roasted peanuts

Directions:
1. Add oil, dish sauce, soy, ginger, garlic, sugar sriracha, coriander and ¼ cup coriander to a bowl and mix. Add the steak and marinate for 30 minutes
2. Add the steak to the air fryer and cook at 200ºC for about 8 minutes
3. Place the steak on a plate and top with remaining coriander and chopped peanuts
4. Serve with peanut sauce

Fish And Seafood Recipes

Cheesy Salmon-stuffed Avocados

Servings: 2
Cooking Time: 20 Minutes
Ingredients:
- 60ml apple cider vinegar
- 5g granular sugar
- 30g sliced red onions
- 60g cream cheese, softened
- 15ml capers
- 2 halved avocados, pitted
- 115g smoked salmon
- 1/4 tsp dried dill
- 2 cherry tomatoes, halved
- 15ml cilantro, chopped

Directions:
1. Warm the apple cider vinegar and sugar in a saucepan over medium heat. Simmer for 4 minutes until it comes to a boil. Add the sliced red onions and turn off the heat. Allow the onions to sit until they are ready to use. Drain before using.
2. In a small bowl, combine the softened cream cheese and capers. Let the mixture chill in the fridge until you are ready to use.
3. Preheat your air fryer to 180°C (350ºF).
4. Place the halved avocados, cut sides up, in the air fryer basket.
5. Air fry the avocado halves for 4 minutes.
6. Transfer the air-fried avocado halves to 2 plates.
7. Top each avocado half with the cream cheese mixture, smoked salmon, dried dill, drained red onions, halved cherry tomatoes, and chopped cilantro.
8. Serve your Cheesy Salmon-Stuffed Avocados immediately.

Asian-style Salmon Fillets

Servings: 4
Cooking Time: 15 Minutes
Ingredients:
- 15ml sesame oil
- 30ml miso paste
- 30ml tamari
- 30ml soy sauce

- 30ml dark brown sugar
- ½ tsp garlic powder
- ½ tsp ginger powder
- 4 salmon fillets
- 4 cups cooked brown rice
- 4 lemon slices

Directions:

1. Preheat the air fryer to 190°C (375°F).
2. In a bowl, combine all ingredients, except for salmon and cooked rice, to make the marinade.
3. Add 1/3 of the marinade to a shallow dish, submerge salmon fillets, and let them marinate covered in the fridge for 10 minutes. Reserve the remaining marinade.
4. Place the salmon fillets, skin side up, in the greased air fryer basket.
5. Air Fry for 6-8 minutes, turning once during cooking, and brush with the reserved marinade.
6. Divide the cooked rice into serving dishes and top each with a salmon fillet.
7. Pour the remaining marinade on top and serve with lemon slices on the side.

Black Olive & Shrimp Salad

Servings: 4
Cooking Time: 15 Minutes
Ingredients:

- 450g cleaned shrimp, deveined
- 120ml olive oil
- 4 garlic cloves, minced
- 1 tbsp balsamic vinegar
- 1/4 tsp cayenne pepper
- 1/4 tsp dried basil
- 1/4 tsp salt
- 1/4 tsp onion powder
- 1 tomato, diced
- 30g black olives

Directions:

1. Preheat your air fryer to 193°C (380°F).
2. In a bowl, combine the olive oil, minced garlic, balsamic vinegar, cayenne pepper, dried basil, salt, and onion powder.
3. Divide the diced tomatoes and black olives evenly between 4 small ramekins.
4. Place the cleaned and deveined shrimp on top of the tomatoes and olives in the ramekins.

5. Pour a quarter of the oil mixture over each of the ramekins, evenly distributing it over the shrimp.
6. Bake in the preheated air fryer for 6-8 minutes or until the shrimp are cooked through.
7. Serve and enjoy your delicious Black Olive & Shrimp Salad!

Breaded Parmesan Perch

Servings: 5
Cooking Time: 15 Minutes
Ingredients:

- 30g grated Parmesan
- 1/2 tsp salt
- 1/4 tsp paprika
- 1 tbsp chopped dill
- 1 tsp dried thyme
- 2 tsp Dijon mustard
- 2 tbsp bread crumbs
- 4 ocean perch fillets
- 1 lemon, quartered
- 2 tbsp chopped cilantro

Directions:

1. Preheat your air fryer to 200°C (400°F).
2. In a wide bowl, combine the salt, paprika, pepper, dill, mustard, thyme, Parmesan, and bread crumbs.
3. Coat all sides of the perch fillets evenly in the breading mixture.
4. Grease the air fryer basket to prevent sticking, then transfer the breaded perch fillets into the basket.
5. Air fry for 8 minutes or until the outside is golden and the inside is cooked through. You may want to check the fillets after 4-5 minutes to ensure they are cooking evenly.
6. Garnish the cooked perch fillets with lemon wedges and sprinkle them with chopped cilantro.
7. Serve your delicious Breaded Parmesan Perch and enjoy!

Cajun Flounder Fillets

Servings: 2
Cooking Time: 5 Minutes
Ingredients:

- 2 115g skinless flounder fillets
- 2 teaspoons peanut oil
- 1 teaspoon purchased or homemade Cajun dried seasoning blend (see note below)

Directions:

1. Preheat your air fryer to 200°C (400°F).
2. Drizzle the peanut oil over the flounder fillets, then gently rub the oil in with your clean, dry fingers.
3. Sprinkle the Cajun seasoning blend evenly over both sides of the fillets.
4. Once your air fryer reaches the desired temperature, place the flounder fillets in the basket. If you are cooking more than one fillet, ensure they do not touch, although they can be close together depending on the basket's size.
5. Air-fry the fillets undisturbed for 5 minutes or until they are lightly browned and cooked through.
6. Use a nonstick-safe spatula to transfer the cooked fillets to a serving platter or individual plates.
7. Serve your Cajun Flounder Fillets immediately.

Asparagus & Salmon Spring Rolls

Servings: 4
Cooking Time: 30 Minutes
Ingredients:

- 225g salmon fillets
- 5ml toasted sesame oil
- 1 onion, sliced
- 8 rice paper wrappers
- 4 asparagus spears, thinly sliced
- 1 carrot, shredded
- 80ml chopped parsley
- 60ml chopped fresh basil

Directions:

1. Preheat the air fryer to 190°C (375°F).
2. Lay the salmon in the air fryer basket and drizzle with toasted sesame oil. Add the sliced onion.
3. Air Fry for 8-10 minutes until the salmon flakes easily with a fork, and the onion becomes soft.
4. Pour warm water into a shallow bowl. One at a time, wet the rice paper wrappers and place them on a clean work surface.
5. Place an eighth of the salmon/onion mixture on each wrapper, along with asparagus, shredded carrot, parsley, and basil.
6. Fold the wrappers and roll them up, sealing the ingredients inside.
7. Air Fry in the air fryer for 7-9 minutes or until the spring rolls become crispy and golden.
8. Serve hot.

Coconut Jerk Shrimp

Servings: 3
Cooking Time: 8 Minutes
Ingredients:

- 1 Large egg white(s)
- 5ml Purchased or homemade jerk dried seasoning blend (see the headnote)
- 90g Plain panko bread crumbs (gluten-free, if a concern)
- 90g Unsweetened shredded coconut
- 12 Large shrimp (20–25 per pound), peeled and deveined
- Coconut oil spray

Directions:

1. Preheat your air fryer to 190°C (375°F).
2. Whisk the egg white(s) and jerk seasoning blend in a bowl until foamy. Add the shrimp and toss well to coat evenly.
3. Mix the bread crumbs and shredded coconut on a dinner plate until well combined. Use kitchen tongs to pick up a shrimp, letting the excess egg white mixture slip back into the bowl. Set the shrimp in the bread-crumb mixture. Turn several times to coat evenly and thoroughly. Set on a cutting board and continue coating the remainder of the shrimp.
4. Lightly coat all the shrimp on both sides with coconut oil spray. Set them in the air fryer basket in one layer with as much space between them as possible. You can even stand some up along the basket's wall in some models.
5. Air-fry undisturbed for 6 minutes, or until the coating is lightly browned. If the air fryer is at 180°C (360°F), you may need to add 2 minutes to the cooking time.
6. Use clean kitchen tongs to transfer the shrimp to a wire rack. Cool for only a minute or two before serving.

Fish Nuggets With Broccoli Dip

Servings: 4
Cooking Time: 40 Minutes
Ingredients:

- 450 grams cod fillets, cut into chunks
- 360 grams broccoli florets
- 30 grams grated Parmesan
- 3 garlic cloves, peeled
- 45 ml sour cream
- 30 ml lemon juice
- 30 ml olive oil

- 2 egg whites
- 120 grams panko breadcrumbs
- 5 ml dried dill
- Salt and pepper to taste

Directions:

1. Preheat the air fryer to 200°C (400°F).

2. Place the broccoli and garlic in the greased frying basket of the air fryer. Air Fry for 5-7 minutes or until the broccoli is tender. Remove the cooked broccoli and garlic to a blender.

3. Add sour cream, lemon juice, olive oil, and ½ teaspoon of salt to the blender with the broccoli and garlic. Process until smooth, then set the sauce aside.

4. Beat the egg whites until frothy in a shallow bowl.

5. On a plate, combine the panko breadcrumbs, grated Parmesan, dried dill, pepper, and the remaining ½ teaspoon of salt.

6. Dip the cod fillets in the egg whites, then coat them in the breadcrumb mixture, pressing to ensure they are evenly coated.

7. Place half of the coated cod fillets in the air fryer basket and spray them with cooking oil.

8. Air Fry for 6-8 minutes or until the fish is cooked through and golden brown.

9. Repeat the process with the remaining fish nuggets.

10. Serve the Fish Nuggets with the Broccoli Dip and enjoy!

Honey Pecan Shrimp

Servings: 4
Cooking Time: 10 Minutes

Ingredients:

- 60 grams cornstarch
- 3.75 milliliters sea salt, divided
- 1.25 milliliters pepper
- 2 egg whites
- 90 grams finely chopped pecans
- 450 grams raw, peeled, and deveined shrimp
- 60 milliliters honey
- 30 milliliters mayonnaise

Directions:

1. In a small bowl, whisk together the cornstarch, 2.5 milliliters (1/2 teaspoon) of sea salt, and the pepper.

2. In a second bowl, whisk the egg whites until they become soft and frothy (they don't need to be whipped to peaks).

3. In a third bowl, mix together the pecans and the remaining 1.25 milliliters (1/4 teaspoon) of sea salt.

4. Pat the shrimp dry with paper towels. Working in small batches, dip the shrimp into the cornstarch, then into the egg whites, and finally into the pecans, ensuring the shrimp are coated with pecans.

5. Preheat the air fryer to 165°C (330°F).

6. Place the coated shrimp inside the air fryer basket and lightly spray them with cooking spray.

7. Cook for 5 minutes, toss the shrimp, and continue cooking for another 5 minutes or until they are cooked through and crispy.

8. While the shrimp are cooking, place the honey in a microwave-safe bowl and microwave for 30 seconds. Whisk in the mayonnaise until smooth and creamy.

9. Pour the honey sauce into a serving bowl.

10. Once the shrimp are done, add them to the serving bowl while they are hot, and toss to coat with the honey sauce.

11. Serve the honey pecan shrimp immediately.

Chinese Fish Noodle Bowls

Servings: 4
Cooking Time: 40 Minutes

Ingredients:

- 1 can (432g) crushed pineapple, drained
- 1 shallot, minced
- 2 tbsp chopped cilantro
- 2 ½ tsp lime juice
- 1 tbsp honey
- Salt and pepper to taste
- 340g grated red cabbage
- 60g chopped green beans
- 2 grated baby carrots
- ½ tsp granulated sugar
- 30ml mayonnaise
- 1 clove garlic, minced
- 225g cooked rice noodles
- 10ml sesame oil
- 5g sesame seeds
- 4 cod fillets
- 5g Chinese five-spice

Directions:

1. Preheat your air fryer to 180°C (350°F).

2. Combine the drained pineapple, minced shallot, 2 tbsp of chopped cilantro, honey, 2 ½ tsp of lime juice, salt, and black pepper in a bowl. Cover the salsa and let it chill in the fridge until ready to use.

3. In another bowl, mix the grated red cabbage, chopped green beans, grated baby carrots, granulated sugar, remaining lime juice, mayonnaise, minced garlic, salt, and pepper. Cover the coleslaw and chill it in the fridge until ready to use.

4. In a separate bowl, toss the cooked rice noodles with sesame oil, stirring occasionally to prevent sticking.

5. Sprinkle the cod fillets with salt and Chinese five-spice.

6. Place the seasoned cod fillets in the greased frying basket of the air fryer.

7. Air Fry for 10 minutes until the fish is opaque and flakes easily with a fork.

8. Divide the cooked noodles into 4 bowls.

9. Top each bowl with the pineapple salsa, coleslaw, and air-fried cod.

10. Serve immediately, sprinkled with an additional tablespoon of cilantro and sesame seeds.

Catalan Sardines With Romesco Sauce

Servings: 2
Cooking Time: 15 Minutes
Ingredients:
- 2 cans skinless, boneless sardines in oil, drained
- 120ml warmed romesco sauce
- 120ml bread crumbs

Directions:
1. Preheat your air fryer to 180°C (350ºF).
2. In a shallow dish, place the bread crumbs.
3. Roll the drained sardines in the bread crumbs to coat them evenly.
4. Grease the air fryer basket to prevent sticking, then place the breaded sardines in the basket.
5. Air fry for 6 minutes, turning the sardines once during cooking to ensure they are crispy and evenly cooked.
6. Serve your Catalan Sardines with Romesco Sauce, and use the warmed romesco sauce as a dipping or drizzling sauce.

Cheesy Tuna Tower

Servings: 2
Cooking Time: 15 Minutes
Ingredients:
- 60g grated mozzarella
- 1 can tuna in water
- 60ml mayonnaise
- 10ml yellow mustard
- 15ml minced dill pickle
- 15ml minced celery
- 15ml minced green onion
- Salt and pepper to taste
- 4 tomato slices
- 8 avocado slices

Directions:
1. Preheat your air fryer to 180°C (350ºF).
2. In a bowl, combine the drained tuna, mayonnaise, yellow mustard, minced dill pickle, minced celery, minced green onion, salt, and pepper to taste. Mix well.
3. Cut a piece of parchment paper to fit the bottom of the air fryer basket.
4. Place the tomato slices on the parchment paper in a single layer and top each tomato slice with 2 avocado slices.
5. Divide the tuna salad mixture evenly over the avocado slices.
6. Sprinkle grated mozzarella cheese on top of each tuna tower.
7. Place the towers in the air fryer basket.
8. Air fry for 4 minutes until the cheese starts to brown.
9. Serve your Cheesy Tuna Towers while they are warm.

Better Fish Sticks

Servings: 3
Cooking Time: 8 Minutes
Ingredients:
- 90g Seasoned Italian-style dried bread crumbs (gluten-free, if needed)
- 15g Finely grated Parmesan cheese
- 285g Skinless cod fillets, cut lengthwise into 2.5cm-wide pieces
- 45ml Regular or low-fat mayonnaise (not fat-free; gluten-free, if needed)
- Vegetable oil spray

Directions:

1. Preheat the air fryer to 200°C (400°F).
2. Mix the bread crumbs and grated Parmesan cheese in a shallow soup bowl or a small pie plate.
3. Coat the fish fillet sticks completely with the mayonnaise, then dip them one by one in the bread-crumb mixture, turning and pressing gently to ensure an even and thorough coating. Coat each stick on all sides with vegetable oil spray.
4. Place the fish sticks in the air fryer basket with at least 0.6 cm (¼ inch) between them.
5. Air-fry undisturbed for 8 minutes, or until they are golden brown and crisp.
6. Use a nonstick-safe spatula to gently transfer the fish sticks from the basket to a wire rack. Allow them to cool for only a minute or two before serving.

Garlic-butter Lobster Tails

Servings: 2
Cooking Time: 20 Minutes
Ingredients:
- 2 lobster tails
- 15 milliliters melted butter
- 2.5 milliliters Old Bay Seasoning
- 2.5 milliliters garlic powder
- 15 milliliters chopped parsley
- 2 lemon wedges

Directions:
1. Preheat the air fryer to 200°C (400°F).
2. Using kitchen shears, cut down the middle of each lobster tail on the softer side. Carefully run your finger between the lobster meat and the shell to loosen the meat.
3. Place the lobster tails in the air fryer basket, cut sides up, and air fry for 4 minutes.
4. After 4 minutes, rub the lobster tails with melted butter, garlic powder, and Old Bay seasoning.
5. Continue to air fry for an additional 4 minutes.
6. Garnish with chopped parsley and serve with lemon wedges.
7. Enjoy your garlic-butter lobster tails!

Bbq Fried Oysters

Servings: 2
Cooking Time: 30 Minutes
Ingredients:
- 60g all-purpose flour
- 120ml barbecue sauce
- 125g bread crumbs
- 225g shelled raw oysters
- 1 lemon
- 15ml chopped parsley

Directions:
1. Preheat the air fryer to 200°C (400°F).
2. In a bowl, place the all-purpose flour.
3. In another bowl, pour the barbecue sauce.
4. In a third bowl, add the breadcrumbs.
5. Roll the shelled raw oysters in the flour, shaking off any excess flour.
6. Dip the floured oysters in the barbecue sauce, shaking off any excess sauce.
7. Dredge the sauced oysters in the breadcrumbs.
8. Place the oysters in the greased air fryer basket.
9. Air Fry for 8 minutes, flipping once during cooking.
10. Sprinkle with chopped parsley and squeeze lemon juice to serve.

Lime Halibut Parcels

Servings: 4
Cooking Time: 45 Minutes
Ingredients:
- 1 lime, sliced
- 4 halibut fillets
- 5 milliliters dried thyme
- Salt and pepper to taste
- 1 shredded carrot
- 1 red bell pepper, sliced
- 120 milliliters sliced celery
- 30 milliliters butter

Directions:
1. Preheat the air fryer to 200°C (400°F).
2. Tear off four 35-centimeter lengths of parchment paper and fold each piece in half crosswise.
3. Place the lime slices in the center of half of each piece of paper, then top with a halibut fillet.
4. Sprinkle each fillet with dried thyme, salt, and pepper. Top each fillet with 1/4 of the shredded carrots, red bell pepper, and sliced celery. Add a dab of butter.
5. Fold the parchment paper in half and crimp the edges all around to enclose the halibut and vegetables.
6. Place one parchment bundle in the air fryer basket, add a raised rack, and then add another bundle.
7. Air fry for 12-14 minutes or until the bundles puff up and the fish flakes easily with a fork.

8. Carefully open the parchment bundles, but be cautious as hot steam will be released.

9. Repeat the process for the second batch of parchment bundles.

Coconut Shrimp With Plum Sauce

Servings: 2
Cooking Time: 30 Minutes
Ingredients:
- 225 grams raw shrimp, peeled
- 2 eggs
- 50 grams breadcrumbs
- 1 tsp red chili powder
- 2 tbsp dried coconut flakes
- Salt and pepper to taste
- 120 ml plum sauce

Directions:
1. Preheat your air fryer to 180°C (350°F).
2. In a bowl, whisk the eggs and season with a pinch of salt and pepper.
3. Dip the shrimp into the beaten eggs, ensuring they are fully coated.
4. In another bowl, combine the breadcrumbs, coconut flakes, red chili powder, and a bit more salt and pepper. Mix until everything is evenly blended.
5. Coat each shrimp in the breadcrumb mixture, pressing the mixture onto the shrimp to make sure they are well coated.
6. Place the coated shrimp in the foil-lined frying basket of your air fryer.
7. Air fry the shrimp for 14-16 minutes, shaking the basket halfway through the cooking time to ensure even cooking.
8. While the shrimp are cooking, warm the plum sauce in a small saucepan over low heat or in a microwave.
9. Once the shrimp are golden brown and crispy, remove them from the air fryer.
10. Serve the coconut shrimp with the plum sauce for dipping.
11. Enjoy your delicious Coconut Shrimp with Plum Sauce!

Holiday Lobster Salad

Servings: 2
Cooking Time: 20 Minutes
Ingredients:
- 2 lobster tails
- 60 milliliters mayonnaise
- 10 milliliters lemon juice
- 1 stalk celery, sliced
- 10 milliliters chopped chives
- 10 milliliters chopped tarragon
- Salt and pepper to taste
- 2 tomato slices
- 4 cucumber slices
- 1 avocado, diced

Directions:
1. Preheat the air fryer to 200°C (400°F).
2. Using kitchen shears, cut down the middle of each lobster tail on the softer side. Carefully run your finger between the lobster meat and the shell to loosen the meat.
3. Place the lobster tails, cut sides up, in the air fryer basket, and air fry for 8 minutes.
4. Transfer the lobster tails to a large plate and let them cool for 3 minutes until they are easy to handle. Then, pull the lobster meat from the shell and roughly chop it.
5. In a bowl, combine the chopped lobster, mayonnaise, lemon juice, sliced celery, chopped chives, chopped tarragon, salt, and pepper.
6. Divide the lobster mixture between 2 medium plates and top with tomato slices, cucumber slices, and diced avocado.
7. Serve immediately.

Mahi Mahi With Cilantro-chili Butter

Servings: 4
Cooking Time: 20 Minutes
Ingredients:
- Salt and pepper to taste
- 4 mahi-mahi fillets
- 30 grams butter, melted
- 2 garlic cloves, minced
- 1.25 milliliters chili powder
- 1.25 milliliters lemon zest
- 5 grams ginger, minced
- 5 milliliters Worcestershire sauce
- 15 milliliters lemon juice
- 15 grams chopped cilantro

Directions:

1. Preheat the air fryer to 190°C (375°F).

2. Combine melted butter, Worcestershire sauce, minced garlic, salt, lemon juice, minced ginger, black pepper, lemon zest, and chili powder in a small bowl.

3. Place the mahi-mahi fillets on a large plate, then spread the seasoned butter mixture on top of each fillet.

4. Arrange the fish in a single layer in the parchment-lined air fryer basket.

5. Air fry for 6 minutes, then carefully flip the fish. Air fry for another 6-7 minutes until the fish is flaky and cooked through.

6. Serve immediately, sprinkled with chopped cilantro.

Mahi-mahi "burrito" Fillets

Servings: 3
Cooking Time: 10 Minutes
Ingredients:

*   1 large egg white
*   90 grams crushed corn tortilla chips (gluten-free, if needed)
*   5 grams chile powder
*   3 skinless mahi-mahi fillets (approximately 140 grams each)
*   90 grams canned refried beans
*   Vegetable oil spray

Directions:

1. Preheat the air fryer to 200°C (400°F).

2. Set up and fill two shallow soup plates or small pie plates on your counter: one with the egg white, beaten until foamy, and one with the crushed tortilla chips.

3. Gently rub 1/2 teaspoon of chile powder on each side of each fillet.

4. Spread 1 tablespoon of refried beans over both sides and the edges of a fillet. Dip the fillet in the egg white, turning to coat it on both sides. Let any excess egg white slip back into the rest, then set the fillet in the crushed tortilla chips. Turn several times, pressing gently to coat it evenly. Coat the fillet on all sides with the vegetable oil spray, then set it aside. Prepare the remaining fillet(s) in the same way.

5. When the air fryer reaches the desired temperature, place the fillets in the basket with as much air space between them as possible. Air-fry undisturbed for 10 minutes, or until they are crisp and browned.

6. Use a nonstick-safe spatula to transfer the fillets to a serving platter or plates. Allow them to cool for only a minute or so, then serve hot.

Fish And "chips"

Servings: 2
Cooking Time: 10 Minutes
Ingredients:

*   120 grams flour
*   2.5 ml paprika
*   1.25 ml ground white pepper (or freshly ground black pepper)
*   1 egg
*   60 ml mayonnaise
*   480 grams salt & vinegar kettle cooked potato chips, coarsely crushed
*   340 grams cod
*   Tartar sauce
*   Lemon wedges

Directions:

1. Set up a dredging station. Combine the flour, paprika, and pepper in a shallow dish. In a second shallow dish, combine the egg and mayonnaise. Place the crushed potato chips in a third shallow dish.

2. Cut the cod into 6 pieces.

3. Dredge each piece of cod in the flour mixture, then dip it into the egg and mayonnaise mixture, and finally, place it into the crushed potato chips. Ensure all sides of the fish are covered, and pat the chips gently onto the fish to make them stick well.

4. Preheat the air fryer to 190°C (370°F).

5. Place the coated fish fillets into the air fry basket. It's okay if a couple of pieces slightly overlap or rest on top of other fillets to fit everything in the basket.

6. Air-fry for 10 minutes, gently turning the fish over halfway through the cooking time.

7. Transfer the cooked fish to a platter and serve with tartar sauce and lemon wedges.

British Fish & Chips

Servings: 4
Cooking Time: 40 Minutes
Ingredients:

*   2 peeled russet potatoes, thinly sliced
*   1 egg white
*   1 tbsp lemon juice
*   80g ground almonds
*   2 bread slices, crumbled
*   1/2 tsp dried basil

- 4 haddock fillets

Directions:

1. Preheat your air fryer to 200°C (390°F).

2. Lay the thinly sliced potato rounds in the air fryer basket and air fry for 11-15 minutes, turning the fries a couple of times during cooking to ensure even crispiness.

3. While the fries are cooking, whisk together the egg white and lemon juice in a bowl.

4. On a plate, combine the ground almonds, breadcrumbs, and dried basil.

5. One at a time, dip the haddock fillets into the egg mixture and then coat them in the almond and breadcrumb mixture.

6. Place the breaded fish fillets on a wire rack while the fries continue to cook.

7. Preheat your oven to 180°C (350°F).

8. After the fries are done in the air fryer, transfer them to a pan and place them in the preheated oven to keep warm.

9. Put the breaded fish fillets in the air fryer basket and air fry for 10-14 minutes or until they are cooked through, golden, and crispy.

10. Serve your British Fish & Chips with the fries.

Cajun-seasoned Shrimp

Servings: 2

Cooking Time: 15 Minutes

Ingredients:

- 450g shelled tail-on shrimp, deveined
- 2 teaspoons grated Parmesan cheese
- 28g butter, melted
- 1 teaspoon cayenne pepper
- 1 teaspoon garlic powder
- 2 teaspoons Cajun seasoning
- 1 tablespoon lemon juice

Directions:

1. Preheat your air fryer to 180°C (350ºF).

2. In a bowl, toss the shrimp with the melted butter, cayenne pepper, garlic powder, and Cajun seasoning until they are well coated.

3. Place the seasoned shrimp in the greased air fryer basket.

4. Air fry for 6 minutes, flipping the shrimp once during cooking to ensure even cooking.

5. Transfer the cooked shrimp to a plate.

6. Squeeze lemon juice over the shrimp and stir in the grated Parmesan cheese.

7. Serve your Cajun-Seasoned Shrimp immediately.

Buttery Lobster Tails

Servings: 4

Cooking Time: 6 Minutes

Ingredients:

- 4 170-225g shell-on raw lobster tails
- 2 tablespoons butter, melted and cooled
- 1 teaspoon lemon juice
- 1/2 teaspoon finely grated lemon zest
- 1/2 teaspoon garlic powder
- 1/2 teaspoon table salt
- 1/2 teaspoon ground black pepper

Directions:

1. Preheat your air fryer to 190°C (375°F).

2. To butterfly the lobster tails, place a tail on a cutting board with the convex side of the shell facing up. Use kitchen shears to cut a line down the middle of the shell from the larger end to the smaller end. Cut only through the shell, not the meat below, and stop before reaching the back fins. Gently pry open the shell, keeping it intact. Use your clean fingers to separate the meat from the sides and bottom of the shell, leaving it attached to the shell at the back near the fins. Pull the meat up and out of the shell through the cut line, laying the meat on top of the shell. Close the shell as best as you can under the meat. Make two equidistant cuts down the meat from the larger end to near the smaller end, each about 1/4 inch deep, for the classic restaurant look on the plate. Repeat this procedure with the remaining tails.

3. In a small bowl, stir together the melted butter, lemon juice, lemon zest, garlic powder, salt, and pepper until well combined.

4. Brush this butter and spice mixture over the lobster meat set atop the shells.

5. Once your air fryer reaches the desired temperature, place the lobster tails shell side down in the basket with as much space between them as possible.

6. Air-fry the tails undisturbed for 6 minutes, or until the lobster meat has pink streaks over it and is firm.

7. Use kitchen tongs to transfer the cooked lobster tails to a wire rack.

8. Allow them to cool for only a minute or two before serving.

Baltimore Crab Cakes

Servings: 4
Cooking Time: 35 Minutes
Ingredients:

- 225g lump crabmeat, shells discarded
- 30ml mayonnaise
- ½ tsp yellow mustard
- ½ tsp lemon juice
- 7.5g minced shallot
- 60ml bread crumbs
- 1 egg
- Salt and pepper to taste
- 4 poached eggs
- 120ml béchamel sauce
- 10g chopped chives
- 1 lemon, cut into wedges

Directions:

1. Preheat the air fryer to 200°C (400°F).
2. In a bowl, combine all ingredients, except for the eggs, sauce, and chives, to form a mixture.
3. Shape the mixture into 4 patties.
4. Place the crab cakes in the greased air fryer basket.
5. Air Fry for 10 minutes, flipping once during cooking.
6. Transfer the crab cakes to a serving dish.
7. Top each crab cake with 1 poached egg, drizzle with béchamel sauce, and sprinkle with chives.
8. Serve with lemon wedges on the side.
9. Enjoy your Baltimore Crab Cakes!

Fried Scallops

Servings: 3
Cooking Time: 6 Minutes
Ingredients:

- 115 grams All-purpose flour or tapioca flour
- 1 Large egg, well beaten
- 240 grams Corn flake crumbs (gluten-free, if needed)
- Up to 2 teaspoons Cayenne pepper
- 1 teaspoon Celery seeds
- 1 teaspoon Table salt
- 450 grams Sea scallops
- Vegetable oil spray

Directions:

1. Preheat the air fryer to 200°C (400°F).
2. Set up and fill three shallow soup plates or small pie plates on your counter: one for the flour; one for the beaten egg; and one for the corn flake crumbs, mixed with the cayenne pepper, celery seeds, and salt until well combined.
3. One by one, dip a scallop in the flour, turning it to coat thoroughly. Gently shake off any excess flour, then dip the scallop in the beaten egg, turning it to coat all sides. Allow any excess egg to drip off, then place the scallop in the corn flake mixture. Turn it several times, pressing gently to ensure an even coating all around. Generously coat the scallop with vegetable oil spray, then set it aside on a cutting board. Repeat this process for the remaining scallops.
4. Place the coated scallops in the air fryer basket with as much air space between them as possible, ensuring they do not touch.
5. Air-fry undisturbed for 6 minutes, or until the scallops are lightly browned and firm.
6. Use kitchen tongs to gently transfer the scallops to a wire rack. Allow them to cool for only a minute or two before serving.

Easy Asian-style Tuna

Servings: 4
Cooking Time: 25 Minutes
Ingredients:

- 1 jalapeño pepper, minced
- 1/2 tsp Chinese five-spice
- 4 tuna steaks
- 1/2 tsp toasted sesame oil
- 2 garlic cloves, grated
- 1 tbsp grated fresh ginger
- Black pepper to taste
- 30 ml lemon juice

Directions:

1. Preheat the air fryer to 190°C (380°F).
2. Drizzle the toasted sesame oil over the tuna steaks and allow them to marinate while you prepare the marinade.
3. In a bowl, combine the minced jalapeño, grated garlic, grated ginger, Chinese five-spice powder, black pepper, and lemon juice to create the marinade.
4. Brush the marinade mixture onto the tuna steaks, ensuring they are evenly coated. Let them sit for 10 minutes to absorb the flavors.
5. Place the marinated tuna steaks in the air fryer basket.

6. Air fry the tuna for 6-11 minutes or until it is cooked through and flakes easily when pressed with a fork.

7. Serve the Asian-Style Tuna steaks warm.

French Grouper Nicoise

Servings: 4

Cooking Time: 20 Minutes

Ingredients:

- 4 grouper fillets
- Salt to taste
- 2.5 ml ground cumin
- 3 garlic cloves, minced
- 1 tomato, sliced
- 60 ml sliced Nicoise olives
- 60 ml dill, chopped
- 1 lemon, juiced
- 60 ml olive oil

Directions:

1. Preheat the air fryer to 193°C (380°F).

2. Sprinkle the grouper fillets with salt and ground cumin.

3. Arrange the seasoned fillets on the greased frying basket.

4. Top the fillets with minced garlic, tomato slices, sliced Nicoise olives, and chopped fresh dill.

5. Drizzle lemon juice and olive oil over the fillets.

6. Bake in the air fryer for 10-12 minutes or until the grouper fillets are cooked through and flaky.

7. Serve your French Grouper Nicoise and enjoy!

Holiday Shrimp Scampi

Servings: 4

Cooking Time: 25 Minutes

Ingredients:

- 680 grams peeled shrimp, deveined
- 1 milliliter lemon pepper seasoning
- 6 garlic cloves, minced
- 5 milliliters salt
- 2.5 milliliters grated lemon zest
- 45 milliliters fresh lemon juice
- 45 milliliters sunflower oil
- 45 milliliters butter
- 10 milliliters fresh thyme leaves
- 1 lemon, cut into wedges

Directions:

1. Preheat the air fryer to 200°C (400°F).

2. In a cake pan, combine the shrimp and minced garlic. Sprinkle with salt and lemon pepper seasoning. Toss to coat.

3. Add the grated lemon zest, fresh lemon juice, sunflower oil, and butter to the shrimp mixture in the cake pan.

4. Place the cake pan in the air fryer basket.

5. Bake for 10-13 minutes, stirring once during cooking, until the shrimp are no longer pink.

6. Sprinkle the cooked shrimp with fresh thyme leaves.

7. Serve hot with lemon wedges on the side.

Maple Balsamic Glazed Salmon

Servings: 4

Cooking Time: 10 Minutes

Ingredients:

- 4 (6-ounce) fillets of salmon
- Salt and freshly ground black pepper
- Vegetable oil
- 60ml (1/4 cup) pure maple syrup
- 3 tablespoons balsamic vinegar
- 1 teaspoon Dijon mustard

Directions:

1. Preheat the air fryer to 200°C (400°F).

2. Season the salmon fillets with salt and freshly ground black pepper.

3. Spray or brush the bottom of the air fryer basket with vegetable oil and place the salmon fillets inside.

4. Air-fry the salmon for 5 minutes.

5. While the salmon is air-frying, combine the maple syrup, balsamic vinegar, and Dijon mustard in a small saucepan over medium heat. Stir to blend well. Allow the mixture to simmer, stirring occasionally. It should start to thicken slightly.

6. Brush the glaze on the salmon fillets and air-fry for an additional 5 minutes. The salmon should feel firm to the touch when finished, and the glaze should be nicely browned on top.

7. Brush a little more glaze on top before removing the salmon from the air fryer.

8. Serve the Maple Balsamic Glazed Salmon with your choice of side dishes, such as rice and vegetables or a green salad.

Buttered Swordfish Steaks

Servings: 4
Cooking Time: 30 Minutes
Ingredients:

- 4 swordfish steaks
- 2 eggs, beaten
- 85g melted butter
- 120g breadcrumbs
- Black pepper to taste
- 1 tsp dried rosemary
- 1 tsp dried marjoram
- 1 lemon, cut into wedges

Directions:

1. Preheat your air fryer to 180°C (350°F).
2. In a bowl, thoroughly stir together the beaten eggs and melted butter.
3. In a separate bowl, combine the breadcrumbs, rosemary, marjoram, and black pepper.
4. Dip each swordfish steak into the beaten egg and butter mixture, ensuring they are well coated.
5. Coat the egg-covered steaks with the breadcrumb mixture, pressing it onto the fish to create a crust.
6. Place the coated swordfish steaks in the air fryer basket.
7. Air fry for 12-14 minutes, turning the steaks once during cooking to ensure they are cooked through and the crust is toasted and crispy.
8. Serve the Buttered Swordfish Steaks with lemon wedges.

Vegetarians Recipes

Bite-sized Blooming Onions

Servings: 4
Cooking Time: 35 Minutes + Cooling Time
Ingredients:

- 450g cipollini onions
- 120g flour
- 1 tsp salt
- ½ tsp paprika
- 1 tsp cayenne pepper
- 2 eggs
- 2 tbsp milk

Directions:

1. Preheat your air fryer to 190°C (375°F).
2. Carefully peel the cipollini onions and cut about 1.3 cm (½ inch) off the stem ends, and trim the root ends.
3. Place the onions root-side down on the cutting surface and cut them into quarters, making sure not to cut all the way to the bottom.
4. Further divide each quarter into 2 sections, and gently pull the wedges apart without breaking them.
5. In a shallow bowl, combine the flour, salt, paprika, and cayenne pepper.
6. In a separate shallow bowl, beat the eggs with the milk until well combined.
7. Dip each onion piece into the flour mixture, ensuring it is coated evenly, then dip it into the egg mixture, and finally back into the flour mixture. Shake off any excess flour.
8. Place the coated onions in the air fryer basket, cut-side up.
9. Lightly spray the onions with cooking oil.
10. Air fry the onions for 10-15 minutes, or until they become crispy on the outside and tender on the inside.
11. Allow the Bite-Sized Blooming Onions to cool for about 10 minutes before serving.

Falafel

Servings: 4

Cooking Time: 10 Minutes

Ingredients:

- 1 can (400g) garbanzo beans (chickpeas), drained and rinsed
- 1 clove garlic, chopped
- 1 cup chopped parsley
- 1/2 cup chopped dill
- 1/2 teaspoon ground cumin
- 1/2 teaspoon ground coriander
- 1 teaspoon salt
- 30g sesame seeds
- 60g breadcrumbs

Directions:

1. Preheat the air fryer to 180°C (350°F).

2. Pat the garbanzo beans dry with a towel. In a food processor, place the beans, garlic, parsley, dill, cumin, coriander, and salt. Blend for 2 minutes, scraping down the sides of the food processor every 30 seconds.

3. In a small bowl, mix together the breadcrumbs and sesame seeds. Working one at a time and using a cookie scoop or approximately 2 tablespoons, form a patty about 1.3cm (1/2 inch) thick and round. Dredge the patties in the breadcrumb mixture.

4. Place the falafel in the air fryer basket, making sure they don't overlap. Spray with cooking spray and cook for 6 minutes, flip them over, and cook for another 4 to 6 minutes. Cook in batches as needed.

Quick-to-make Quesadillas

Servings: 4

Cooking Time: 30 Minutes

Ingredients:

- 340g goat cheese
- 30 ml vinegar
- 15 ml Taco seasoning
- 1 ripe avocado, pitted
- 4 scallions, finely sliced
- 30 ml lemon juice
- 4 flour tortillas
- 60 ml hot sauce
- 120 ml Alfredo sauce
- 16 cherry tomatoes, halved

Directions:

1. Preheat your air fryer to 200°C (400°F).

2. Slice the goat cheese into 4 pieces and set them aside.

3. In a bowl, whisk together the vinegar and Taco seasoning until well combined. Submerge each cheese slice into the vinegar mixture and air-fry for 12 minutes until they become crisp, turning them once. Let them cool slightly before cutting into 1.25 cm (0.5-inch) thick strips.

4. In another bowl, mash the avocado with a fork. Stir in the finely sliced scallions and lemon juice, and set aside.

5. Lay one tortilla on a flat surface. Cut from one edge to the center, creating four quadrants.

6. Spread ¼ of the avocado mixture on one quadrant, 15 ml (1 tbsp) of hot sauce on the next quadrant, and finally, 60 ml (2 tbsp) of Alfredo sauce on the other half.

7. Top the non-sauce half with ¼ of the cherry tomatoes and ¼ of the goat cheese strips.

8. To fold, start with the avocado quadrant, folding each over the next one until you create a stacked triangle.

9. Repeat the process with the remaining tortillas.

10. Air-fry the quesadillas for 5 minutes until they are crispy, turning them once.

11. Serve your Quick-To-Make Quesadillas while they're warm. Enjoy!

Eggplant Parmesan

Servings: 4

Cooking Time: 10 Minutes

Ingredients:

- 1 medium, round eggplant, sliced into 1.25cm-thick rounds
- 10ml salt, divided
- 60g all-purpose flour
- 5ml dried thyme
- 2 eggs
- 120g breadcrumbs
- 2.5ml dried oregano
- 60g grated Parmesan cheese, plus more for garnish
- 480ml marinara sauce
- 30ml chopped parsley, for garnish

Directions:

1. Place the eggplant slices on a baking sheet lined with paper towels or a tea towel in a single layer. Sprinkle the eggplant with 7.5ml (5 teaspoons) of the salt. Place another layer of paper towels or a tea towel on top and then add weights like pots or plates on top of that. The

idea is to press the bitterness out of the eggplant. Let the eggplant sit for 30 minutes.

2. Meanwhile, in a medium bowl, mix together the flour, 1.25ml (1/4 teaspoon) of salt, and the dried thyme.

3. In a second bowl, whisk the eggs.

4. In a third bowl, mix together the remaining 1.25ml (1/4 teaspoon) of salt, breadcrumbs, dried oregano, and 60g (1/4 cup) of Parmesan cheese.

5. Preheat the air fryer to 190°C (370°F).

6. Remove the towels and rinse the eggplant slices. Pat the slices dry and begin breading the eggplant. Working with 1 slice at a time, first dip it into the flour mixture and shake off the excess flour. Next, dip it into the eggs. Finally, dredge the eggplant in the breadcrumb mixture. Repeat with the remaining eggplant slices.

7. Place a single layer of eggplant slices in the air fryer basket and spray liberally with cooking spray. Cook for 5 minutes, flip them over, spray with cooking spray, and cook for another 5 minutes.

8. Meanwhile, heat the marinara sauce in a saucepan until warm.

9. To serve, plate the eggplant rounds and spoon the marinara sauce over each round. Sprinkle with Parmesan cheese and parsley for garnish. Serve hot or at room temperature.

Cheesy Eggplant Rounds

Servings: 4
Cooking Time: 35 Minutes
Ingredients:
- 1 eggplant, peeled
- 2 eggs
- 60g all-purpose flour
- 90g bread crumbs
- 30g grated Swiss cheese
- Salt and pepper to taste
- 180ml tomato passata
- 60g shredded Parmesan cheese
- 60g shredded mozzarella cheese

Directions:
1. Preheat your air fryer to 200°C (400°F).

2. Slice the peeled eggplant into 1.25cm (½-inch) rounds. Set them aside.

3. Set out three small bowls:

4. In the first bowl, add the all-purpose flour.

5. In the second bowl, beat the eggs.

6. In the third bowl, mix the bread crumbs, 2 tablespoons of grated Swiss cheese, salt, and pepper.

7. Dip each eggplant round in the flour, then dredge it in the beaten egg, and finally coat it with the bread crumb mixture.

8. Arrange the coated eggplant rounds in the greased air fryer basket.

9. Spray the eggplant rounds with cooking oil.

10. Bake for 7 minutes.

11. Top each eggplant round with 1 teaspoon of tomato passata, ½ tablespoon each of shredded Parmesan and shredded mozzarella cheese.

12. Continue cooking until the cheese melts, which should take about 2-3 minutes.

13. Serve your Cheesy Eggplant Rounds warm and enjoy!

Kale & Lentils With Crispy Onions

Servings: 4
Cooking Time: 40 Minutes
Ingredients:
- 450 grams cooked red lentils
- 1 onion, sliced into rings
- 120 grams kale, steamed
- 3 garlic cloves, minced
- Juice and zest of 1/2 lemon
- 2 teaspoons cornflour (cornstarch)
- 1 teaspoon dried oregano
- Salt and pepper to taste
- Cooking oil spray

Directions:
1. Preheat your air fryer to 200°C (390°F). Place the sliced onion rings in the greased air fryer basket, making sure not to overlap them. Spray them lightly with cooking oil and season with salt.

2. Air fry the onion rings for 14-16 minutes, stirring twice during the cooking process, until they become crispy and crunchy.

3. While the onions are frying, place the kale and cooked lentils in a pan over medium heat. Stir until they are heated through.

4. Remove the pan from heat and add the minced garlic, lemon juice, cornflour, salt, lemon zest, dried oregano, and black pepper. Stir the mixture well to combine.

5. Divide the kale and lentil mixture into bowls.

6. Top each bowl with the crispy onion rings.

7. Serve and enjoy your delicious Kale & Lentils with Crispy Onions!

Cheese Ravioli

Servings: 4
Cooking Time: 9 Minutes
Ingredients:
- 1 egg
- 60ml milk
- 120g breadcrumbs
- 2 teaspoons Italian seasoning
- 0.3g ground rosemary
- 1.25g basil
- 1.25g parsley
- 255g uncooked cheese ravioli
- 30g flour
- Oil for misting or cooking spray

Directions:
1. Preheat your air fryer to 200°C (390°F).
2. In a medium bowl, beat together the egg and milk.
3. In a large plastic bag, mix together the breadcrumbs, Italian seasoning, ground rosemary, basil, and parsley.
4. Place all the cheese ravioli and the flour in a bag or a bowl with a lid and shake to coat the ravioli with flour.
5. Working with a handful at a time, drop the floured ravioli into the egg wash. Remove the ravioli, letting excess drip off, and place them in the bag with breadcrumbs.
6. When all the ravioli are in the breadcrumb bag, shake well to coat all the pieces.
7. Dump enough ravioli into the air fryer basket to form one layer. Mist them with oil or use cooking spray.
8. Dump the remaining ravioli on top of the first layer and mist them with oil.
9. Cook for 5 minutes, then shake well and spray with oil. Break apart any ravioli that may be stuck together and spray any spots you missed the first time.
10. Cook for an additional 4 minutes or until the ravioli puff up and become crispy golden brown.

Mushroom Bolognese Casserole

Servings: 4
Cooking Time: 20 Minutes
Ingredients:
- 240 ml canned diced tomatoes
- 2 garlic cloves, minced
- 1 teaspoon onion powder
- 3/4 teaspoon dried basil
- 3/4 teaspoon dried oregano
- 240 grams chopped mushrooms
- 450 grams cooked spaghetti

Directions:
1. Preheat your air fryer to 200°C (400°F).
2. In a baking pan, whisk together the diced tomatoes and their juices, minced garlic, onion powder, dried basil, dried oregano, and chopped mushrooms.
3. Cover the baking pan with aluminum foil and place it in the air fryer. Bake for 6 minutes.
4. Carefully slide out the pan from the air fryer and add the cooked spaghetti to the tomato and mushroom mixture. Stir to coat the spaghetti.
5. Cover the pan again with aluminum foil and return it to the air fryer. Bake for an additional 3 minutes, until the casserole is heated through and bubbly.
6. Serve your Mushroom Bolognese Casserole and enjoy!

Chive Potato Pierogi

Servings: 4
Cooking Time: 55 Minutes
Ingredients:
- 2 boiled potatoes, mashed
- Salt and pepper to taste
- 1 tsp cumin powder
- 30ml sour cream
- 30g grated Parmesan
- 2 tbsp chopped chives
- 1 tbsp chopped parsley
- 160g flour
- 1/4 tsp garlic powder
- 180ml Greek yogurt
- 1 egg

Directions:
1. In a bowl, combine the mashed potatoes along with sour cream, cumin, parsley, chives, pepper, and salt. Stir until the mixture is slightly chunky.
2. In a large bowl, mix the flour, salt, and garlic powder. Stir in the Greek yogurt until it comes together as a sticky dough. Knead the dough in the bowl for about 2-3 minutes until it becomes smooth.
3. In a small bowl, whisk the egg and add 5ml (1 teaspoon) of water to create an egg wash.

4. Roll out the dough on a lightly floured work surface to a thickness of 6mm (1/4 inch). Cut out 12 circles using a cookie cutter.

5. Preheat the air fryer to 180°C (350°F).

6. Divide the potato mixture and Parmesan cheese evenly between the dough circles. Brush the edges of the circles with the egg wash and fold the dough over the filling to create half-moon shapes. Use a fork to crimp the edges and seal the pierogies.

7. Place the pierogies in the greased air fryer basket. Air fry for 8-10 minutes, turning the pierogies once, until they turn golden on the outside.

8. Serve the Chive Potato Pierogi while they are still warm. Enjoy your meal!

Fennel Tofu Bites

Servings: 4
Cooking Time: 35 Minutes
Ingredients:
- 75ml vegetable broth
- 2 tablespoons tomato sauce
- 2 teaspoons soy sauce
- 1 tablespoon nutritional yeast
- 1 teaspoon Italian seasoning
- 1 teaspoon granulated sugar
- 1 teaspoon grated ginger
- 1/2 teaspoon fennel seeds
- 1/2 teaspoon garlic powder
- Salt and pepper to taste
- 400g firm tofu, cubed
- 85g bread crumbs
- 1 teaspoon Italian seasoning
- 2 teaspoons toasted sesame seeds
- 240ml marinara sauce, warm

Directions:
1. In a large bowl, whisk together the vegetable broth, soy sauce, grated ginger, tomato sauce, nutritional yeast, Italian seasoning, sugar, fennel seeds, garlic powder, salt, and black pepper. Toss the tofu cubes in this mixture to coat. Let them marinate, covered in the fridge, for 30 minutes, tossing them once during marination.

2. Preheat the air fryer to 180°C (350°F).

3. In a bowl, mix the breadcrumbs, Italian seasoning, and salt. Strain the marinade from the tofu cubes and dredge them in the breadcrumb mixture until coated.

4. Place the tofu cubes in the greased air fryer basket and air fry for 10 minutes, turning them once to ensure even cooking.

5. Serve the Fennel Tofu Bites sprinkled with sesame seeds and marinara sauce on the side.

Rigatoni With Roasted Onions, Fennel, Spinach, And Lemon Pepper Ricotta

Servings: 2
Cooking Time: 13 Minutes
Ingredients:
- 1 red onion, roughly chopped into large chunks
- 2 teaspoons olive oil, divided
- 1 bulb fennel, sliced ¼-inch thick
- 180g ricotta cheese
- 1½ teaspoons finely chopped lemon zest, plus more for garnish
- 5 ml lemon juice
- Salt and freshly ground black pepper
- 225g (½ pound) dried rigatoni pasta
- 90g baby spinach leaves

Directions:
1. Bring a large stockpot of salted water to a boil on the stovetop and Preheat the air fryer to 200°C (400°F).

2. While the water is coming to a boil, toss the chopped onion in 5 ml of olive oil and transfer it to the air fryer basket. Air-fry at 200°C (400°F) for 5 minutes.

3. Toss the sliced fennel with 5 ml of olive oil and add this to the air fryer basket with the onions. Continue to air-fry at 200°C (400°F) for 8 minutes, shaking the basket a few times during the cooking process.

4. Combine the ricotta cheese, lemon zest and juice, ¼ teaspoon of salt and freshly ground black pepper in a bowl and stir until smooth.

5. Add the dried rigatoni to the boiling water and cook according to the package directions. When the pasta is cooked al dente, reserve one cup of the pasta water and drain the pasta into a colander.

6. Place the spinach in a serving bowl and immediately transfer the hot pasta to the bowl, wilting the spinach. Add the roasted onions and fennel and toss together. Add a little pasta water to the dish if it needs moistening.

7. Then, dollop the lemon pepper ricotta cheese on top and nestle it into the hot pasta. Garnish with more lemon zest if desired.

Effortless Mac 'n' Cheese

Servings: 4
Cooking Time: 15 Minutes
Ingredients:

- 240ml heavy cream
- 240ml milk
- 120g mozzarella cheese
- 10g grated Parmesan cheese
- 450g cooked elbow macaroni

Directions:

1. Preheat the air fryer to 200°C (400°F).
2. In a bowl, whisk together the heavy cream, milk, mozzarella cheese, and grated Parmesan cheese until the mixture is smooth.
3. Stir in the cooked elbow macaroni and pour the mixture into a baking dish.
4. Cover the dish with foil.
5. Bake in the air fryer for 6 minutes.
6. Remove the foil and continue to bake until the mac 'n' cheese is cooked through and bubbly, which should take an additional 3-5 minutes.
7. Serve the Effortless Mac 'n' Cheese while it's still warm.

Italian-style Fried Cauliflower

Servings: 4
Cooking Time: 35 Minutes
Ingredients:

- 2 eggs
- 80g all-purpose flour
- 2.5ml Italian seasoning
- 60g bread crumbs
- 5ml garlic powder
- 15ml grated Parmesan cheese
- Salt and pepper to taste
- 1 head cauliflower, cut into florets
- 2.5ml ground coriander

Directions:

1. Preheat the air fryer to 190°C (370°F).
2. Set out 3 small bowls. In the first bowl, mix the flour with Italian seasoning. In the second bowl, beat the eggs. In the third bowl, combine the bread crumbs, garlic powder, grated Parmesan cheese, ground coriander, salt, and pepper.
3. Dip the cauliflower florets in the flour mixture, then dredge them in the beaten eggs, and finally coat them in the bread crumb mixture.
4. Place a batch of cauliflower in the greased air fryer basket and spray them with cooking oil.
5. Air fry for 10-12 minutes, shaking the basket once during cooking, until the cauliflower turns golden.
6. Serve the Italian-Style Fried Cauliflower warm.

Basil Green Beans

Servings: 4
Cooking Time: 15 Minutes
Ingredients:

- 680 grams green beans, trimmed
- 15 ml olive oil
- 15 ml fresh basil, chopped
- Garlic salt to taste

Directions:

1. Preheat the air fryer to 200°C (400°F).
2. In a large bowl, coat the green beans with olive oil.
3. Combine the fresh basil and garlic salt with the green beans, ensuring they are well coated.
4. Place the seasoned green beans in the air fryer basket.
5. Air Fry for 7-9 minutes, shaking the basket once during cooking until the beans begin to brown.
6. Serve the basil green beans warm and enjoy!

Asparagus, Mushroom And Cheese Soufflés

Servings: 3
Cooking Time: 21 Minutes
Ingredients:

- Butter
- Grated Parmesan cheese
- 3 button mushrooms, thinly sliced
- 8 spears asparagus, sliced 1.25 cm long
- 1 teaspoon olive oil
- 1 tablespoon butter
- 20 grams plain flour
- Pinch of paprika
- Pinch of ground nutmeg
- Salt and freshly ground black pepper
- 120 ml milk

- 60 grams grated Gruyère cheese or other Swiss cheese (about 60 grams)
- 2 eggs, separated

Directions:

1. Grease three 6-ounce ramekins with butter and dust them with grated Parmesan cheese. (Butter the ramekins and then coat the butter with Parmesan by shaking it around in the ramekin and dumping out any excess.)

2. Preheat the air fryer to 200°C (400°F).

3. Toss the mushrooms and asparagus in a bowl with the olive oil. Transfer the vegetables to the air fryer and air-fry for 7 minutes, shaking the basket once or twice to redistribute the ingredients while they cook.

4. While the vegetables are cooking, make the soufflé base. Melt the butter in a saucepan on the stovetop over medium heat. Add the flour, stir, and cook for a minute or two. Add the paprika, nutmeg, salt, and pepper. Whisk in the milk and bring the mixture to a simmer to thicken. Remove the pan from the heat and add the cheese, stirring to melt. Let the mixture cool for just a few minutes and then whisk the egg yolks in, one at a time. Stir in the cooked mushrooms and asparagus. Let this soufflé base cool.

5. In a separate bowl, whisk the egg whites to the soft peak stage (the point at which the whites can almost stand up on the end of your whisk). Fold the whipped egg whites into the soufflé base, adding a little at a time.

6. Preheat the air fryer to 165°C (330°F).

7. Transfer the batter carefully to the buttered ramekins, leaving about 1.25 cm at the top. Place the ramekins into the air fryer basket and air-fry for 14 minutes. The soufflés should have risen nicely and be brown on top. Serve immediately. Enjoy your asparagus, mushroom, and cheese soufflés!

Golden Fried Tofu

Servings: 4
Cooking Time: 20 Minutes
Ingredients:

- 30g flour
- 30g cornstarch
- 1 teaspoon garlic powder
- 1/4 teaspoon onion powder
- Salt and pepper to taste
- 400g firm tofu, cubed
- 2 tablespoons cilantro, chopped
- Cooking oil spray

Directions:

1. Preheat the air fryer to 200°C (390°F).

2. In a bowl, combine the flour, cornstarch, salt, garlic powder, onion powder, and black pepper. Stir well.

3. Place the tofu cubes into the flour mixture and toss to coat them evenly.

4. Spray the coated tofu with cooking oil and place them in a single layer in the greased air fryer basket.

5. Air fry for 14-16 minutes, flipping the tofu pieces once during cooking, until they are golden and crunchy.

6. Top the fried tofu with freshly chopped cilantro and serve immediately.

Quinoa & Black Bean Stuffed Peppers

Servings: 4
Cooking Time: 30 Minutes
Ingredients:

- 120 ml vegetable broth
- 120 ml quinoa
- 1 can black beans
- 120 ml diced red onion
- 1 garlic clove, minced
- 2.5 ml salt
- 2.5 ml ground cumin
- 1.25 ml paprika
- 1.25 ml ancho chili powder
- 4 bell peppers, any color
- 120 ml grated cheddar
- 60 ml chopped cilantro
- 120 ml red enchilada sauce

Directions:

1. Add vegetable broth and quinoa to a small saucepan over medium heat. Bring to a boil, then cover and let it simmer for 5 minutes. Turn off the heat.

2. Preheat your air fryer to 180°C (350°F).

3. Transfer quinoa to a medium bowl and stir in black beans, red onion, red enchilada sauce, ancho chili powder, garlic, salt, cumin, and paprika.

4. Cut the top 0.6 cm (0.25 inch) off the bell peppers. Remove the seeds and membranes.

5. Scoop the quinoa filling into each pepper and top with cheddar cheese.

6. Transfer the stuffed peppers to the air fryer basket and air-fry for 10 minutes until the peppers are soft and the filling is heated through.

7. Garnish with cilantro.

8. Serve your Quinoa & Black Bean Stuffed Peppers warm along with salsa. Enjoy!

Breaded Avocado Tacos

Servings: 3

Cooking Time: 20 Minutes

Ingredients:

- 2 tomatoes, diced
- 30g diced red onion
- 1 jalapeño, finely diced
- 15ml lime juice
- 1 tsp lime zest
- 30g chopped cilantro
- 1 tsp salt
- 1 egg
- 30ml milk
- 120g breadcrumbs
- 30g almond flour
- 1 avocado, sliced into fries
- 6 flour tortillas
- 120g coleslaw mix

Directions:

1. In a bowl, combine the diced tomatoes, finely diced jalapeño, red onion, lime juice, lime zest, chopped cilantro, and salt. Cover the pico de gallo and refrigerate it until you're ready to use it.

2. Preheat your air fryer to 190°C (375°F).

3. In a small bowl, beat the egg and milk together.

4. In another bowl, combine the breadcrumbs and almond flour.

5. Dip the avocado slices into the egg mixture, ensuring they are coated, and then dredge them in the mixed almond flour and breadcrumbs until they are well coated.

6. Place the breaded avocado slices in the greased air fryer basket.

7. Air fry the avocado slices for 5 minutes or until they become crispy and golden.

8. Assemble the tacos by adding 2 avocado fries to each flour tortilla.

9. Top each taco with coleslaw mix.

10. Serve your Breaded Avocado Tacos immediately, accompanied by the chilled pico de gallo.

Honey Pear Chips

Servings: 4

Cooking Time: 30 Minutes

Ingredients:

- 2 firm pears, thinly sliced
- 15ml lemon juice
- 2.5ml ground cinnamon
- 5ml honey

Directions:

1. Preheat the air fryer to 190°C (380°F).

2. Arrange the thinly sliced pear slices on the parchment-lined cooking basket.

3. Drizzle the pear slices with lemon juice and honey, and sprinkle them with ground cinnamon.

4. Air fry for 6-8 minutes, shaking the basket once during cooking, until the pear slices turn golden.

5. Allow the Honey Pear Chips to cool.

6. Serve immediately or store them in an airtight container for up to 2 days.

Cheddar-bean Flautas

Servings: 4

Cooking Time: 15 Minutes

Ingredients:

- 8 corn tortillas
- 1 can refried beans
- 100g shredded cheddar cheese
- 240ml guacamole

Directions:

1. Preheat your air fryer to 200°C (390°F).

2. Wet the corn tortillas with water to make them pliable.

3. Spray the air fryer basket with oil, and stack the tortillas inside.

4. Air fry the tortillas for 1 minute to make them slightly crispy.

5. Remove the tortillas to a flat surface, laying them out individually.

6. Scoop an equal amount of refried beans in a line down the center of each tortilla.

7. Top the beans with shredded cheddar cheese.

8. Roll the sides of the tortillas over the filling and place them seam-side down in the greased air fryer basket.

9. Air fry the flautas for 7 minutes or until the tortillas are golden and crispy.

10. Serve your Cheddar-Bean Flautas immediately, topped with guacamole.

Corn And Pepper Jack Chile Rellenos With Roasted Tomato Sauce

Servings: 3
Cooking Time: 30 Minutes
Ingredients:

- 3 Poblano peppers
- 150g all-purpose flour
- Salt and freshly ground black pepper
- 2 eggs, lightly beaten
- 100g plain breadcrumbs
- Olive oil, in a spray bottle
- Sauce
- 200g cherry tomatoes
- 1 Jalapeño pepper, halved and seeded
- 1 clove garlic
- 25g red onion, broken into large pieces
- 15ml olive oil
- Salt, to taste
- 2 tablespoons chopped fresh cilantro
- Filling
- 15ml olive oil
- 25g red onion, finely chopped
- 1 teaspoon minced garlic
- 150g corn kernels, fresh or frozen
- 200g grated pepper jack cheese

Directions:

1. Start by roasting the peppers. Preheat the air fryer to 200°C (400°F). Place the peppers into the air fryer basket and air-fry at 200°C (400°F) for 10 minutes, turning them over halfway through the cooking time. Remove the peppers from the basket and cover loosely with foil.

2. While the peppers are cooling, make the roasted tomato sauce. Place all sauce ingredients except for the cilantro into the air fryer basket and air-fry at 200°C (400°F) for 10 minutes, shaking the basket once or twice. When the sauce ingredients have finished air-frying, transfer everything to a blender or food processor and blend or process to a smooth sauce, adding a little warm water to get the desired consistency. Season to taste with salt, add the cilantro and set aside.

3. While the sauce ingredients are cooking in the air fryer, make the filling. Heat a skillet on the stovetop over medium heat. Add the olive oil and sauté the red onion and garlic for 4 to 5 minutes. Transfer the onion and garlic to a bowl, stir in the corn and cheese, and set aside.

4. Set up a dredging station with three shallow dishes. Place the flour, seasoned with salt and pepper, in the first shallow dish. Place the eggs in the second dish, and fill the third shallow dish with the breadcrumbs. When the peppers have cooled, carefully slice into one side of the pepper to create an opening. Pull the seeds out of the peppers and peel away the skins, trying not to tear the pepper. Fill each pepper with some of the corn and cheese filling and close the pepper up again by folding one side of the opening over the other. Carefully roll each pepper in the seasoned flour, then into the egg and finally into the breadcrumbs to coat on all sides, trying not to let the pepper fall open. Spray the peppers on all sides with a little olive oil.

5. Air-fry two peppers at a time at 175°C (350°F) for 6 minutes. Turn the peppers over and air-fry for another 4 minutes. Serve the peppers warm on a bed of the roasted tomato sauce.

Pizza Margherita With Spinach

Servings: 4
Cooking Time: 50 Minutes
Ingredients:

- 120 ml pizza sauce
- 5 ml dried oregano
- 5 ml garlic powder
- 1 pizza dough
- 240 ml baby spinach
- 120 ml mozzarella cheese

Directions:

1. Preheat your air fryer to 200°C (400°F).

2. Whisk together the pizza sauce, dried oregano, and garlic powder in a bowl. Set aside.

3. Divide the pizza dough into 4 equal portions and roll out each portion into a 15 cm (6-inch) round pizza.

4. Place one pizza crust in the air fryer basket. Spread 60 ml (1/4 cup) of the sauce over the crust, then scatter 60 ml (1/4 cup) of spinach, and finally top with 60 ml (1/4 cup) of mozzarella cheese.

5. Grill the pizza for 8 minutes or until it becomes golden brown and the crust is crispy.

6. Repeat the process with the remaining pizza crusts.

7. Serve your Pizza Margherita with Spinach immediately. Enjoy!

Cheesy Eggplant Lasagna

Servings: 4
Cooking Time: 40 Minutes
Ingredients:

- 95g chickpea flour
- 120ml milk
- 45ml lemon juice
- 15ml chili sauce
- 10ml allspice
- 120g panko breadcrumbs
- 1 eggplant, sliced
- 475ml jarred tomato sauce
- 120g ricotta cheese
- 80g mozzarella cheese

Directions:

1. Preheat your air fryer to 200°C (400°F).
2. In a bowl, whisk together the chickpea flour, milk, lemon juice, chili sauce, and allspice until you have a smooth batter. Set this aside.
3. On a plate, spread out the panko breadcrumbs.
4. Submerge each eggplant slice into the batter, shaking off any excess, and then dip it into the breadcrumbs until it's well coated.
5. Place the coated eggplant slices in the air fryer and cook for 10 minutes, turning them once during cooking. Let them cool slightly.
6. Spread 2 tablespoons of tomato sauce at the bottom of a baking pan.
7. Lay a single layer of eggplant slices on top of the tomato sauce.
8. Scatter ricotta cheese over the eggplant slices and top with more tomato sauce.
9. Repeat the layering process until you've used up all the ingredients.
10. Scatter mozzarella cheese on top of the lasagna.
11. Bake at 175°C (350°F) for 10 minutes or until the eggplants are cooked and the cheese turns golden brown.
12. Serve your Cheesy Eggplant Lasagna immediately.

Meatless Kimchi Bowls

Servings: 4
Cooking Time: 20 Minutes
Ingredients:

- 400 grams canned chickpeas
- 1 carrot, julienned
- 6 scallions, sliced
- 1 zucchini, diced
- 30 ml coconut aminos
- 10 ml sesame oil
- 5 ml rice vinegar
- 10 grams granulated sugar
- 15 ml gochujang
- 1/4 teaspoon salt
- 120 grams kimchi
- 10 grams roasted sesame seeds

Directions:

1. Preheat your air fryer to 175°C (350°F).
2. In a baking pan, combine all the ingredients except for the kimchi, 2 scallions, and sesame seeds.
3. Place the pan in the frying basket of the air fryer.
4. Air Fry for 6 minutes.
5. After 6 minutes, add the kimchi to the mixture and cook for an additional 2 minutes.
6. Divide the cooked mixture between 4 bowls.
7. Garnish each bowl with the remaining sliced scallions and roasted sesame seeds.
8. Serve immediately and enjoy your Meatless Kimchi Bowls!

Cheesy Veggie Frittata

Servings: 2
Cooking Time: 65 Minutes
Ingredients:

- 115g Bella mushrooms, chopped
- 30g halved grape tomatoes
- 40g baby spinach
- 30g chopped leeks
- 1 baby carrot, chopped
- 4 eggs
- 60g grated cheddar cheese
- 15ml milk
- 1 teaspoon garlic powder
- 1/4 teaspoon dried oregano
- Salt and pepper to taste

Directions:

1. Preheat your air fryer to 150°C (300°F).
2. Crack the eggs into a bowl and beat them with a fork or whisk.
3. Mix in the remaining ingredients until well combined.
4. Pour the mixture into a greased cake pan.

5. Place the pan into the air fryer basket.

6. Bake for 20-23 minutes or until the eggs are set in the center.

7. Remove the frittata from the air fryer.

8. Cut it into halves and serve.

Spiced Vegetable Galette

Servings: 4

Cooking Time: 30 Minutes

Ingredients:

- 60ml cooked eggplant, chopped
- 60ml cooked zucchini, chopped
- 1 refrigerated pie crust
- 2 eggs
- 60ml milk
- Salt and pepper to taste
- 1 red chili, finely sliced
- 60ml tomato, chopped
- 120g shredded mozzarella cheese

Directions:

1. Preheat the air fryer to 180°C (360°F).

2. In a baking dish, add the crust and press firmly. Trim off any excess edges. Poke a few holes in the crust.

3. Beat the eggs in a bowl. Stir in the milk, half of the cheese, eggplant, zucchini, tomato, red chili, salt, and pepper. Mix well.

4. Transfer the mixture to the baking dish with the pie crust and spread it evenly.

5. Place the baking dish in the air fryer and bake for 15 minutes or until the galette is firm and almost crusty.

6. Slide the basket out and top the galette with the remaining cheese.

7. Cook for an additional 5 minutes, or until the galette is golden brown.

8. Let it cool slightly, then serve.

Roasted Vegetable Lasagna

Servings: 6

Cooking Time: 55 Minutes

Ingredients:

- 1 zucchini, sliced
- 1 yellow squash, sliced
- 225g mushrooms, sliced
- 1 red bell pepper, cut into 5cm strips
- 15ml olive oil
- 475g ricotta cheese
- 190g grated mozzarella cheese, divided
- 1 egg
- 5ml salt
- freshly ground black pepper
- 60ml shredded carrots
- 120g chopped fresh spinach
- 8 lasagna noodles, cooked
- Béchamel Sauce:
- 45g butter
- 45g flour
- 590ml milk
- 60g grated Parmesan cheese
- 2.5ml salt
- freshly ground black pepper
- pinch of ground nutmeg

Directions:

1. Preheat the air fryer to 200°C (400°F).

2. Toss the zucchini, yellow squash, mushrooms, and red pepper in a large bowl with the olive oil and season with salt and pepper. Air-fry for 10 minutes, shaking the basket once or twice while the vegetables cook.

3. While the vegetables are cooking, make the béchamel sauce and cheese filling. Melt the butter in a medium saucepan over medium-high heat on the stovetop. Add the flour and whisk, cooking for a couple of minutes. Add the milk and whisk vigorously until smooth. Bring the mixture to a boil and simmer until the sauce thickens. Stir in the Parmesan cheese and season with the salt, pepper, and nutmeg. Set the sauce aside.

4. Combine the ricotta cheese, 300g of the mozzarella cheese, egg, salt, and pepper in a large bowl and stir until combined. Fold in the carrots and spinach.

5. When the vegetables have finished cooking, build the lasagna. Use a baking dish that is 15cm in diameter and 10cm high. Cover the bottom of the baking dish with a little béchamel sauce. Top with two lasagna noodles, cut to fit the dish and overlapping each other a little. Spoon a third of the ricotta cheese mixture and then a third of the roasted veggies on top of the noodles. Pour 120ml of béchamel sauce on top and then repeat these layers two more times: noodles – cheese mixture – vegetables – béchamel sauce. Sprinkle the remaining mozzarella cheese over the top. Cover the dish with aluminum foil, tenting it loosely so the aluminum doesn't touch the cheese.

6. Lower the dish into the air fryer basket using an aluminum foil sling (fold a piece of aluminum foil into a strip about 5cm wide by 60cm long). Fold the ends of the aluminum foil over the top of the dish before returning the basket to the air fryer. Air-fry for 45 minutes, removing the foil for the last 2 minutes, to slightly brown the cheese on top.

7. Let the lasagna rest for at least 20 minutes to set up a little before slicing into it and serving.

Cheddar Stuffed Portobellos With Salsa

Servings: 4
Cooking Time: 20 Minutes
Ingredients:
- 8 portobello mushrooms
- 80ml salsa
- 120g shredded cheddar cheese
- 2 tablespoons cilantro, chopped

Directions:
1. Preheat your air fryer to 190°C (370°F).
2. Remove the stems from the portobello mushrooms.
3. Divide the salsa between the mushroom caps, spreading it evenly in each cap.
4. Top each mushroom cap with shredded cheddar cheese.
5. Sprinkle chopped cilantro over the cheese.
6. Place the stuffed mushrooms in the greased air fryer basket.
7. Bake the mushrooms in the air fryer for 8-10 minutes or until the cheese is melted and the mushrooms are tender.
8. Let the stuffed portobellos cool slightly before serving.

Basic Fried Tofu

Servings: 4
Cooking Time: 17 Minutes
Ingredients:
- 400 grams extra-firm tofu, drained and pressed
- 1 tablespoon sesame oil
- 2 tablespoons low-sodium soy sauce
- 60 ml rice vinegar
- 1 tablespoon fresh grated ginger
- 1 clove garlic, minced
- 3 tablespoons cornstarch
- 1/4 teaspoon black pepper
- 1/8 teaspoon salt

Directions:
1. Cut the tofu into 16 cubes. Set aside in a glass container with a lid.
2. In a medium bowl, mix the sesame oil, soy sauce, rice vinegar, ginger, and garlic. Pour this mixture over the tofu and secure the lid. Place it in the refrigerator to marinate for an hour.
3. Preheat the air fryer to 180°C (350°F).
4. In a small bowl, mix the cornstarch, black pepper, and salt.
5. Transfer the marinated tofu to a large bowl and discard the leftover marinade. Pour the cornstarch mixture over the tofu and toss until all the pieces are coated.
6. Liberally spray the air fryer basket with olive oil mist and place the tofu pieces inside, ensuring there's enough space between them for even cooking. Cook in batches if necessary.
7. Cook for 15 to 17 minutes, shaking the basket every 5 minutes to ensure the tofu cooks evenly on all sides. When done, the tofu should be crisped and browned on all sides.
8. Remove the tofu from the air fryer basket and serve it warm. Enjoy your basic fried tofu!

Curried Cauliflower

Servings: 2
Cooking Time: 30 Minutes
Ingredients:
- 240ml canned diced tomatoes
- 480ml milk
- 30ml lime juice
- 15ml allspice
- 15ml curry powder
- 5ml ground ginger
- 2.5ml ground cumin
- 340g frozen cauliflower
- 450g cheddar cheese, cubed
- 60ml chopped cilantro

Directions:
1. Preheat the air fryer to 190°C (375°F).
2. In a baking pan, combine the diced tomatoes and their juices, milk, lime juice, allspice, curry powder, ground ginger, and ground cumin.

3. Toss in the frozen cauliflower and cubed cheddar cheese until they are coated with the sauce mixture.

4. Roast for 15 minutes, then stir the mixture, and continue roasting for another 10 minutes until it becomes bubbly and the cauliflower is cooked.

5. Scatter chopped cilantro over the top before serving your Curried Cauliflower.

Rice & Bean Burritos

Servings: 4

Cooking Time: 20 Minutes

Ingredients:

- 1 bell pepper, sliced
- 1/2 red onion, thinly sliced
- 2 garlic cloves, peeled
- 15 ml olive oil
- 240 ml cooked brown rice
- 1 can pinto beans
- 2.5 ml salt
- 1.25 ml chili powder
- 1.25 ml ground cumin
- 1.25 ml smoked paprika
- 15 ml lime juice
- 4 tortillas
- 10 ml grated Parmesan cheese
- 1 avocado, diced
- 60 ml salsa
- 30 ml chopped cilantro

Directions:

1. Preheat the air fryer to 200°C (400°F).

2. Combine bell pepper, onion, garlic, and olive oil. Place in the frying basket and Roast for 5 minutes. Shake and roast for another 5 minutes.

3. Remove the garlic from the basket and mince finely. Add to a large bowl along with brown rice, pinto beans, salt, chili powder, cumin, paprika, and lime juice.

4. Divide the roasted vegetable mixture between the tortillas. Top with rice mixture, Parmesan, avocado, cilantro, and salsa.

5. Fold in the sides, then roll the tortillas over the filling.

6. Serve your delicious Rice & Bean Burritos and enjoy!

Poultry Recipes

Fennel & Chicken Ratatouille

Servings: 4
Cooking Time: 30 Minutes
Ingredients:

- 450g boneless, skinless chicken thighs, cubed
- 2 tbsp grated Parmesan cheese
- 1 eggplant, cubed
- 1 zucchini, cubed
- 1 bell pepper, diced
- 1 fennel bulb, sliced
- 1 tsp salt
- 1 tsp Italian seasoning
- 2 tbsp olive oil
- 1 can diced tomatoes
- 1 tsp pasta sauce
- 2 tbsp basil leaves

Directions:

1. Preheat the air fryer to 200°C.
2. In a bowl, mix the chicken, eggplant, zucchini, bell pepper, fennel, salt, Italian seasoning, and olive oil.
3. Place the chicken mixture in the air fryer basket and Air Fry for 7 minutes.
4. Transfer the cooked mixture to a cake pan.
5. Mix in the diced tomatoes along with their juices and pasta sauce.
6. Air Fry for an additional 8 minutes.
7. Scatter the grated Parmesan cheese and basil leaves over the ratatouille.
8. Serve and enjoy your Fennel & Chicken Ratatouille!

Air Fryer Chicken Thigh Schnitzel

Servings: 4
Cooking Time:xx
Ingredients:

- 300g boneless chicken thighs
- 160g seasoned breadcrumbs
- 1 tsp salt
- ½ tsp ground black pepper
- 30g flour
- 1 egg
- Cooking spray

Directions:

1. Lay the chicken on a sheet of parchment paper and add another on top
2. Use a mallet or a rolling pin to flatten it down
3. Take a bowl and add the breadcrumbs with the salt and pepper
4. Place the flour into another bowl
5. Dip the chicken into the flour, then the egg, and then the breadcrumbs
6. Preheat air fryer to 190°C
7. Place the chicken into the air fryer and spray with cooking oil
8. Cook for 6 minutes

Chicken Breasts Wrapped In Bacon

Servings: 4
Cooking Time: 35 Minutes
Ingredients:

- 60ml mayonnaise
- 60ml sour cream
- 45ml ketchup
- 15ml yellow mustard
- 15ml light brown sugar
- 450g chicken tenders
- 5ml dried parsley
- 8 bacon slices

Directions:

1. Preheat your air fryer to 188°C (370°F).
2. In a bowl, combine the mayonnaise, sour cream, ketchup, mustard, and brown sugar. Mix well and set aside.
3. Sprinkle the chicken tenders with dried parsley.
4. Wrap each chicken tender with a slice of bacon.
5. Place the wrapped chicken tenders in the air fryer basket in a single layer.
6. Air fry the chicken for 18-20 minutes, flipping them once, until the bacon is crisp and the chicken is cooked through.
7. Serve the chicken breasts wrapped in bacon with the sauce.

Coconut Curry Chicken With Coconut Rice

Servings: 4
Cooking Time: 56 Minutes
Ingredients:

- 1 (400g) can coconut milk
- 2 tablespoons green or red curry paste
- Zest and juice of one lime
- 1 clove garlic, minced
- 1 tablespoon grated fresh ginger
- 1 teaspoon ground cumin
- 1 (1.4 to 1.8 kg) chicken, cut into 8 pieces
- Vegetable or olive oil
- Salt and freshly ground black pepper
- Fresh cilantro leaves
- For the rice:
- 250g basmati or jasmine rice
- 250ml water
- 250ml coconut milk
- ½ teaspoon salt
- Freshly ground black pepper

Directions:

1. Make the marinade by combining the coconut milk, curry paste, lime zest and juice, garlic, ginger, and cumin. Coat the chicken on all sides with the marinade and marinate the chicken for 1 hour to overnight in the refrigerator.
2. Preheat the air fryer to 190°C.
3. Brush the bottom of the air fryer basket with oil. Transfer the chicken thighs and drumsticks from the marinade to the air fryer basket, letting most of the marinade drip off. Season to taste with salt and freshly ground black pepper.
4. Air-fry the chicken drumsticks and thighs at 190°C for 12 minutes. Flip the chicken over and continue to air-fry for another 12 minutes. Set aside and air-fry the chicken breast pieces at 190°C for 15 minutes. Turn the chicken breast pieces over and air-fry for another 12 minutes. Return the chicken thighs and drumsticks to the air fryer and air-fry for an additional 5 minutes.
5. While the chicken is cooking, make the coconut rice. Rinse the rice kernels with water and drain well. Place the rice in a medium saucepan with a tight-fitting lid, along with the water, coconut milk, salt, and freshly ground black pepper. Bring the mixture to a boil and then cover, reduce the heat, and let it cook gently for 20 minutes without lifting the lid. When the time is up, lift the lid, fluff with a fork, and set aside.
6. Remove the chicken from the air fryer and serve warm with the coconut rice and fresh cilantro scattered around.

Chicken And Cheese Chimichangas

Servings: 6
Cooking Time:xx
Ingredients:

- 100g shredded chicken (cooked)
- 150g nacho cheese
- 1 chopped jalapeño pepper
- 6 flour tortillas
- 5 tbsp salsa
- 60g refried beans
- 1 tsp cumin
- 0.5 tsp chill powder
- Salt and pepper to taste

Directions:

1. Take a large mixing bowl and add all of the ingredients, combining well
2. Add ⅓ of the filling to each tortilla and roll into a burrito shape
3. Spray the air fryer with cooking spray and heat to 200ºC
4. Place the chimichangas in the air fryer and cook for 7 minutes

Intense Buffalo Chicken Wings

Servings: 2
Cooking Time: 40 Minutes
Ingredients:

- 8 chicken wings
- 120ml melted butter
- 2 tbsp Tabasco sauce
- 15ml lemon juice
- 1 tbsp Worcestershire sauce
- 10ml cayenne pepper
- 5ml garlic powder
- 5ml lemon zest
- Salt and pepper to taste

Directions:

1. Preheat the air fryer to 180°C (350°F).

2. In a bowl, combine the melted butter, Tabasco sauce, lemon juice, Worcestershire sauce, cayenne pepper, garlic powder, lemon zest, salt, and pepper. Stir the mixture until well combined.

3. Dip each chicken wing into the mixture, ensuring they are thoroughly coated.

4. Place the coated chicken wings on the foil-lined frying basket in an even layer.

5. Air Fry for 16-18 minutes, shaking the basket several times during cooking to ensure even crisping.

6. Once the chicken wings are crispy brown, remove them from the air fryer and serve your Intense Buffalo Chicken Wings.

Harissa Chicken Wings

Servings: 4
Cooking Time: 25 Minutes
Ingredients:
- 8 whole chicken wings
- 1 tsp garlic powder
- ¼ tsp dried oregano
- 1 tbsp harissa seasoning

Directions:

1. Preheat the air fryer to 200°C (392°F).

2. Season the wings with garlic powder, harissa seasoning, and dried oregano.

3. Place the seasoned wings in the greased frying basket, and lightly spray them with cooking oil.

4. Air fry for 10 minutes, then shake the basket to ensure even cooking.

5. Continue to air fry for an additional 5-7 minutes or until the wings are golden and crispy.

6. Serve the harissa chicken wings while still warm. Enjoy!

Crispy Cordon Bleu

Servings: 4
Cooking Time: 25 Minutes
Ingredients:
- 4 deli ham slices, halved lengthwise
- 2 tbsp grated Parmesan
- 4 chicken breast halves
- Salt and pepper to taste
- 8 Swiss cheese slices
- 1 egg

- 2 egg whites
- 75g bread crumbs
- 1 tsp garlic powder
- 1 tsp onion powder
- 1 tsp mustard powder

Directions:

1. Preheat the air fryer to 200°C.

2. Season the chicken cutlets with salt and pepper.

3. On one cutlet, put a half slice of ham and cheese on the top. Roll the chicken tightly, then set aside.

4. Beat the eggs and egg whites in a shallow bowl.

5. Put the breadcrumbs, Parmesan, garlic, onion, and mustard powder in a second bowl.

6. Dip the cutlet in the egg bowl and then in the crumb mix. Press so that they stick to the chicken.

7. Put the rolls of chicken seam side down in the greased frying basket and Air Fry for 12-14 minutes, flipping once until golden and cooked through.

Grain-free Chicken Katsu

Servings: 4
Cooking Time:xx
Ingredients:
- 125 g/1¼ cups ground almonds
- ½ teaspoon salt
- ½ teaspoon garlic powder
- ½ teaspoon dried parsley
- ½ teaspoon freshly ground black pepper
- ¼ teaspoon onion powder
- ¼ teaspoon dried oregano
- 450 g/1 lb. mini chicken fillets
- 1 egg, beaten
- oil, for spraying/drizzling
- coriander/cilantro leaves, to serve
- KATSU SAUCE
- 1 teaspoon olive oil or avocado oil
- 1 courgette/zucchini (approx. 150 g/5 oz.), finely chopped
- 1 carrot (approx. 100 g/3½ oz.), finely chopped
- 1 onion (approx. 120 g/4½ oz.), finely chopped
- 1 eating apple (approx. 150 g/5 oz.), cored and finely chopped
- 1 teaspoon ground ginger
- 1 teaspoon ground turmeric
- 2 teaspoons ground cumin

- 2 teaspoons ground coriander
- 1½ teaspoons mild chilli/chili powder
- 1 teaspoon garlic powder
- 1½ tablespoons runny honey
- 1 tablespoon soy sauce (gluten-free if you wish)
- 700 ml/3 cups vegetable stock (700 ml/3 cups water with 1½ stock cubes)

Directions:

1. First make the sauce. The easiest way to ensure all the vegetables and apple are finely chopped is to combine them in a food processor. Heat the oil in a large saucepan and sauté the finely chopped vegetables and apple for 5 minutes. Add all the seasonings, honey, soy sauce and stock and stir well, then bring to a simmer and simmer for 30 minutes.

2. Meanwhile, mix together the ground almonds, seasonings and spices. Dip each chicken fillet into the beaten egg, then into the almond-spice mix, making sure each fillet is fully coated. Spray the coated chicken fillets with olive oil (or simply drizzle over).

3. Preheat the air-fryer to 180°C/350°F.

4. Place the chicken fillets in the preheated air-fryer and air-fry for 10 minutes, turning halfway through cooking. Check the internal temperature of the chicken has reached at least 74°C/165°F using a meat thermometer – if not, cook for another few minutes.

5. Blend the cooked sauce in a food processor until smooth. Serve the chicken with the Katsu Sauce drizzled over (if necessary, reheat the sauce gently before serving) and scattered with coriander leaves. Any unused sauce can be frozen.

Lemon Herb Whole Cornish Hen

Servings: 2
Cooking Time: 50 Minutes
Ingredients:

- 1 Cornish hen
- 60ml olive oil
- 30ml lemon juice
- 2 tablespoons sage, chopped
- 2 tablespoons thyme, chopped
- 4 garlic cloves, chopped
- Salt and pepper to taste
- 1 celery stalk, chopped
- 1/2 small onion
- 1/2 lemon, juiced and zested

- 2 tablespoons chopped parsley

Directions:

1. Preheat the air fryer to 190°C (380°F).

2. In a bowl, whisk together the olive oil, lemon juice, chopped sage, chopped thyme, chopped garlic, salt, and pepper.

3. Rub the olive oil and herb mixture over the top and sides of the Cornish hen. Pour any excess mixture inside the cavity of the bird.

4. Stuff the hen's cavity with chopped celery, onion, lemon juice, and lemon zest.

5. Place the seasoned and stuffed Cornish hen in the air fryer frying basket.

6. Roast for 40-45 minutes in the air fryer until the hen is cooked through and the skin is crispy.

7. Cut the Cornish hen in half and serve, garnished with chopped parsley.

Bbq Chicken Tenders

Servings: 6
Cooking Time:xx
Ingredients:

- 300g barbecue flavoured pork rinds
- 200g all purpose flour
- 1 tbsp barbecue seasoning
- 1 egg
- 400g chicken breast tenderloins
- Cooking spray

Directions:

1. Preheat the air fryer to 190°C

2. Place the pork rinds into a food processor and blitz to a breadcrumb consistency, before transferring to a bowl

3. In a separate bowl, combine the flour and barbecue seasoning

4. Beat the egg in a small bowl

5. Take the chicken and first dip into the egg, then the flour, and then the breadcrumbs

6. Place the chicken into the air fryer and spray with cooking spray and cook for about 15 minutes

Chicken Cordon Bleu

Servings: 4
Cooking Time: 20 Minutes
Ingredients:

- 4 small boneless, skinless chicken breasts
- Salt and pepper, to taste
- 4 slices of deli ham
- 4 slices of deli Swiss cheese (approximately 7.5 to 10 cm square)
- 2 tablespoons olive oil
- 2 teaspoons dried marjoram
- ¼ teaspoon paprika

Directions:

1. Begin by carefully slicing each chicken breast horizontally, leaving one edge intact.
2. Lay the chicken breasts open flat and season them with salt and pepper to your liking.
3. On top of each chicken breast, place a slice of ham.
4. Cut the cheese slices in half and position one-half on each chicken breast, reserving the remaining halves for later use.
5. Carefully roll up the chicken breasts to enclose the cheese and ham, securing them in place with toothpicks.
6. In a small bowl, combine the olive oil, dried marjoram, and paprika. Mix well and rub this mixture evenly over the outsides of the chicken breasts.
7. Place the prepared chicken in the air fryer basket and cook at 180°C (360°F) for approximately 20 minutes or until the chicken is thoroughly cooked, and the juices run clear.
8. Remove all toothpicks from the chicken breasts. To avoid any burns, transfer the chicken breasts to a plate to remove the toothpicks safely, and then return them immediately to the air fryer basket.
9. Lastly, add half a cheese slice on top of each chicken breast, and cook for an additional minute or until the cheese has melted and is slightly bubbly.

Chicken And Wheat Stir Fry

Servings: 4
Cooking Time:xx
Ingredients:

- 1 onion
- 1 clove of garlic
- 200g skinless boneless chicken breast halves
- 3 whole tomatoes
- 400ml water
- 1 chicken stock cube
- 1 tbsp curry powder
- 130g wheat berries
- 1 tbsp vegetable oil

Directions:

1. Thinly slice the onion and garlic
2. Chop the chicken and tomatoes into cubes
3. Take a large saucepan and add the water, chicken stock, curry powder and wheat berries, combining well
4. Pour the oil into the air fryer bowl and heat for 5 minutes at 200ºC
5. Add the remaining ingredients and pour the contents into the air fryer
6. Cook for 15 minutes

Chicken Wellington

Servings: 2
Cooking Time: 31 Minutes
Ingredients:

- 2 (140g) boneless, skinless chicken breasts
- 120ml White Worcestershire sauce
- 45g butter
- 120g finely diced onion (about ½ onion)
- 225g button mushrooms, finely chopped
- 60ml chicken stock
- 30ml White Worcestershire sauce (or white wine)
- Salt and freshly ground black pepper
- 15g chopped fresh tarragon
- 2 sheets puff pastry, thawed
- 1 egg, beaten
- Vegetable oil

Directions:

1. Place the chicken breasts in a shallow dish. Pour the White Worcestershire sauce over the chicken coating both sides and marinate for 30 minutes.
2. While the chicken is marinating, melt the butter in a large skillet over medium-high heat on the stovetop. Add the onion and sauté for a few minutes, until it starts to soften. Add the mushrooms and sauté for 5 minutes until the vegetables are brown and soft. Deglaze the skillet with the chicken stock, scraping up any bits from the bottom of the pan. Add the White Worcestershire sauce and simmer for 3 minutes until the mixture reduces and starts to thicken. Season with salt and freshly ground black pepper. Remove the mushroom mixture from the

heat and stir in the fresh tarragon. Let the mushroom mixture cool.

3. Preheat the air fryer to 180°C (360°F).

4. Remove the chicken from the marinade and transfer it to the air fryer basket. Tuck the small end of the chicken breast under the thicker part to shape it into a circle rather than an oval. Pour the marinade over the chicken and air-fry for 10 minutes.

5. Roll out the puff pastry and cut out two 15cm squares. Brush the perimeter of each square with the egg wash. Place half of the mushroom mixture in the center of each puff pastry square. Place the chicken breasts, top side down on the mushroom mixture. Starting with one corner of puff pastry and working in one direction, pull the pastry up over the chicken to enclose it and press the ends of the pastry together in the middle. Brush the pastry with the egg wash to seal the edges. Turn the Wellingtons over and set aside.

6. To make a decorative design with the remaining puff pastry, cut out four 25cm strips. For each Wellington, twist two of the strips together, place them over the chicken breast wrapped in puff pastry, and tuck the ends underneath to seal it. Brush the entire top and sides of the Wellingtons with the egg wash.

7. Preheat the air fryer to 175°C (350°F).

8. Spray or brush the air fryer basket with vegetable oil. Air-fry the chicken Wellingtons for 13 minutes. Carefully turn the Wellingtons over. Air-fry for another 8 minutes. Transfer to serving plates and enjoy your Chicken Wellington!

Cajun Chicken Kebabs

Servings: 4
Cooking Time: 30 Minutes
Ingredients:

- 45ml lemon juice
- 10ml olive oil
- 30ml chopped parsley
- 2.5ml dried oregano
- 2.5ml Cajun seasoning
- 450 grams chicken breasts, cubed
- 240 grams cherry tomatoes
- 1 zucchini, cubed

Directions:

1. Preheat your air fryer to 200°C (400°F).

2. In a bowl, combine the lemon juice, olive oil, chopped parsley, dried oregano, and Cajun seasoning.

3. Toss the cubed chicken in the marinade, ensuring that all pieces are well coated. Allow the chicken to marinate for 10 minutes.

4. Take 8 bamboo skewers and alternate threading the marinated chicken, cherry tomatoes, and cubed zucchini onto the skewers.

5. Use a brush to apply more marinade to the kebabs.

6. Place the kebabs in the air fryer basket.

7. Air fry the kebabs for 15 minutes, turning them once during cooking, or until the chicken is fully cooked through with no pink showing. Discard any leftover marinade.

8. Serve and enjoy your Cajun Chicken Kebabs!

Boss Chicken Cobb Salad

Servings: 2
Cooking Time: 30 Minutes
Ingredients:

- 115 grams cooked bacon, crumbled
- 60ml diced peeled red onion
- 60 grams crumbled blue cheese
- 1 egg
- 15ml honey
- 15ml Dijon mustard
- 2.5ml apple cider vinegar
- 2 chicken breasts, cubed
- 180ml bread crumbs
- Salt and pepper to taste
- 90 grams torn iceberg lettuce
- 40 grams baby spinach
- 120ml ranch dressing
- ½ avocado, diced
- 1 beefsteak tomato, diced
- 1 hard-boiled egg, diced
- 30ml parsley

Directions:

1. Preheat your air fryer to 180°C (350°F).

2. In a bowl, mix the egg, honey, Dijon mustard, and apple cider vinegar. Add the chicken cubes to the mixture and toss to coat. Shake off any excess marinade from the chicken.

3. In another bowl, combine the breadcrumbs, salt, and pepper. Dredge the chicken cubes in this breadcrumb mixture until they are coated evenly.

4. Place the breaded chicken cubes in the greased frying basket of the air fryer.

5. Air fry for 8-10 minutes, tossing the chicken once during cooking to ensure even browning.

6. In a salad bowl, combine the torn iceberg lettuce, baby spinach, and ranch dressing. Toss to coat.

7. Add the cooked chicken, crumbled bacon, diced avocado, diced red onion, crumbled blue cheese, diced beefsteak tomato, diced hard-boiled egg, and parsley to the salad.

8. Serve your Boss Chicken Cobb Salad immediately and enjoy!

Chilean-style Chicken Empanadas

Servings: 4
Cooking Time: 25 Minutes

Ingredients:
- 115g chorizo sausage, casings removed and crumbled
- 15ml olive oil
- 115g chicken breasts, diced
- 30g black olives, sliced
- 5ml chili powder
- 5ml paprika
- 30g raisins
- 4 empanada shells

Directions:
1. Preheat the air fryer to 175°C (350°F).

2. Warm the olive oil in a skillet over medium heat. Sauté the chicken and chorizo, breaking up the chorizo, for 3-4 minutes.

3. Add the raisins, chili powder, paprika, and olives to the skillet. Stir well. Remove the skillet from heat and allow the mixture to cool slightly.

4. Divide the chorizo mixture between the empanada shells and fold them over to cover the filling. Seal the edges with water and press down with a fork to secure.

5. Place the empanadas in the air fryer basket.

6. Bake for 15 minutes, flipping them once during cooking, until they turn golden brown.

7. Serve the Chilean-Style Chicken Empanadas while they are still warm. Enjoy!

Berry-glazed Turkey Breast

Servings: 4
Cooking Time: 1 Hour 25 Minutes

Ingredients:
- 1 bone-in, skin-on turkey breast
- 15ml olive oil
- Salt and pepper to taste
- 240 grams raspberries
- 240 grams chopped strawberries
- 30ml balsamic vinegar
- 30ml melted butter
- 15ml honey mustard
- 5ml dried rosemary

Directions:
1. Preheat your air fryer to 180°C (350°F).

2. Lay the turkey breast skin-side up in the frying basket, brush it with olive oil, and season with salt and pepper.

3. Bake for 55-65 minutes, flipping the turkey twice during cooking to ensure even browning.

4. While the turkey is cooking, prepare the berry glaze. In a blender, combine the raspberries, chopped strawberries, balsamic vinegar, melted butter, honey mustard, and dried rosemary. Blend until the mixture is smooth.

5. Turn the turkey skin-side up inside the fryer and brush it with half of the berry glaze. Bake for an additional 5 minutes.

6. Transfer the remaining berry glaze to a small saucepan and simmer for 3-4 minutes while the turkey continues to cook.

7. Once the turkey is done, allow it to stand for 10 minutes to rest.

8. Carve the turkey and serve it with the remaining berry glaze.

Quick Chicken Nuggets

Servings: 4
Cooking Time:xx

Ingredients:
- 500g chicken tenders
- 25g ranch salad dressing mixture
- 2 tbsp plain flour
- 100g breadcrumbs
- 1 egg, beaten
- Olive oil spray

Directions:
1. Take a large mixing bowl and arrange the chicken inside

2. Sprinkle the seasoning over the top and ensure the chicken is evenly coated

3. Place the chicken to one side for around 10 minutes

4. Add the flour into a resealable bag

5. Crack the egg into a small mixing bowl and whisk

6. Pour the breadcrumbs onto a medium sized plate

7. Transfer the chicken into the resealable bag and coat with the flour, giving it a good shake

8. Remove the chicken and dip into the egg, and then rolling it into the breadcrumbs, coating evenly

9. Repeat with all pieces of the chicken

10. Heat your air fryer to 200ºC

11. Arrange the chicken inside the fryer and add a little olive oil spray to avoid sticking

12. Cook for 4 minutes, before turning over and cooking for another 4 minutes

13. Remove and serve whilst hot

Enchilada Chicken Quesadillas

Servings: 4
Cooking Time: 35 Minutes
Ingredients:

- 300g cooked chicken breasts, shredded
- 1 can diced green chilies, including juice
- 200g grated Mexican cheese blend
- 180ml sour cream
- 2 tsp chili powder
- 1 tsp cumin
- 1 tbsp chipotle sauce
- 1 tsp dried onion flakes
- ½ tsp salt
- 45g butter, melted
- 8 flour tortillas

Directions:

1. In a small bowl, whisk together the sour cream, chipotle sauce, and chili powder. Let it chill in the fridge until ready to use.

2. Preheat the air fryer to 180°C.

3. Mix the chicken, green chilies, cumin, and salt in a bowl. Set aside.

4. Brush one side of a tortilla lightly with melted butter. Layer with 60g of chicken, onion flakes, and 60g of Mexican cheese. Top with a second tortilla and lightly brush with butter on top. Repeat with the remaining ingredients.

5. Place quesadillas, butter side down, in the frying basket of the air fryer. Bake for 3 minutes.

6. Cut them into 6 sections and serve with the cream sauce on the side.

Crispy Chicken Parmesan

Servings: 4
Cooking Time: 12 Minutes
Ingredients:

- 4 skinless, boneless chicken breasts, pounded thin to ¼-inch thickness
- 1 teaspoon salt, divided
- ½ teaspoon black pepper, divided
- 120g flour
- 2 eggs
- 70g panko breadcrumbs
- ½ teaspoon dried oregano
- 50g grated Parmesan cheese

Directions:

1. Pat the chicken breasts with a paper towel. Season the chicken with ½ teaspoon of the salt and ¼ teaspoon of the pepper.

2. In a medium bowl, place the flour.

3. In a second bowl, whisk the eggs.

4. In a third bowl, place the breadcrumbs, oregano, cheese, and the remaining ½ teaspoon of salt and ¼ teaspoon of pepper.

5. Dredge the chicken in the flour and shake off the excess. Dip the chicken into the eggs and then into the breadcrumb mixture. Set the chicken on a plate and repeat with the remaining chicken pieces.

6. Preheat the air fryer to 180°C.

7. Place the chicken in the air fryer basket and spray liberally with cooking spray. Cook for 8 minutes, turn the chicken breasts over, and cook for another 4 minutes. When golden brown, check for an internal temperature of 74°C.

Family Chicken Fingers

Servings: 4
Cooking Time: 30 Minutes
Ingredients:

- 450g chicken breast fingers
- 1 tbsp chicken seasoning
- ½ tsp mustard powder
- Salt and pepper to taste

- 2 eggs
- 100g bread crumbs

Directions:

1. Preheat the air fryer to 200°C.

2. In a large bowl, combine the chicken fingers with chicken seasoning, mustard powder, salt, and pepper; mix well.

3. Set up two small bowls. In one bowl, beat the eggs. In the second bowl, place the bread crumbs.

4. Dip each chicken finger in the beaten eggs, allowing any excess to drip off, then coat it with the bread crumbs.

5. Place the coated chicken fingers in the air fryer basket. Lightly spray them with cooking oil.

6. Air Fry for 8 minutes, shaking the basket once to ensure even cooking, until the chicken fingers are crispy and cooked through.

7. Serve them warm and enjoy your Family Chicken Fingers!

Cheesy Chicken Tenders

Servings: 4
Cooking Time: 25 Minutes

Ingredients:

- 240ml grated Parmesan cheese
- 60ml grated cheddar
- 570 grams chicken tenders
- 1 egg, beaten
- 30ml milk
- Salt and pepper to taste
- 2.5ml garlic powder
- 5ml dried thyme
- 1.25ml shallot powder

Directions:

1. Preheat your air fryer to 200°C (400°F).

2. Stir the beaten egg and milk together until combined.

3. On a plate, mix together the salt, pepper, garlic powder, dried thyme, shallot powder, cheddar cheese, and Parmesan cheese.

4. Dip each chicken tender into the egg mixture, then into the cheese mixture, pressing to coat them evenly.

5. Place the coated chicken tenders in the air fryer frying basket in a single layer. If you have a raised rack, you can use it to cook more at one time.

6. Spray all the chicken tenders with oil.

7. Bake the chicken tenders for 12-16 minutes, flipping them once halfway through cooking.

8. Serve your Cheesy Chicken Tenders while hot.

Classic Chicken Cobb Salad

Servings: 4
Cooking Time: 30 Minutes

Ingredients:

- 115g cooked bacon, crumbled
- 2 chicken breasts, cubed
- 15ml sesame oil
- Salt and pepper to taste
- 4 cups torn romaine lettuce
- 30ml olive oil
- 15ml white wine vinegar
- 2 hard-boiled eggs, sliced
- 2 tomatoes, diced
- 6 radishes, finely sliced
- 30g blue cheese crumbles
- 30g diced red onions
- 1 avocado, diced

Directions:

1. Preheat the air fryer to 180°C (350°F).

2. In a bowl, combine the chicken cubes with sesame oil, salt, and black pepper.

3. Place the seasoned chicken cubes in the air fryer basket and Air Fry for 9 minutes, flipping them once during cooking. Make sure the chicken is thoroughly cooked. Once done, set the chicken aside.

4. In a separate bowl, combine the torn romaine lettuce with olive oil and white wine vinegar. Toss to coat the lettuce.

5. Divide the dressed lettuce between 4 serving bowls.

6. Add the cooked chicken, sliced hard-boiled eggs, crumbled bacon, diced tomatoes, finely sliced radishes, blue cheese crumbles, diced red onions, and diced avocado to each bowl.

7. Serve your Classic Chicken Cobb Salad for a delicious and satisfying meal. Enjoy!

Japanese-inspired Glazed Chicken

Servings: 4
Cooking Time: 25 Minutes
Ingredients:

- 4 chicken breasts
- Chicken seasoning to taste
- Salt and pepper to taste
- 10g grated fresh ginger
- 2 garlic cloves, minced
- 60ml molasses
- 30ml tamari sauce

Directions:

1. Preheat the air fryer to 200°C (400°F).
2. Season the chicken breasts with chicken seasoning, salt, and pepper to taste.
3. Place the seasoned chicken breasts in the greased air fryer frying basket.
4. Air Fry for 7 minutes, then flip the chicken breasts and cook for another 3 minutes or until they are cooked through.
5. While the chicken is cooking, prepare the glaze by combining the grated ginger, minced garlic, molasses, and tamari sauce in a saucepan over medium heat.
6. Cook the sauce for 4 minutes or until it thickens.
7. Transfer all of the cooked chicken breasts to a serving dish.
8. Drizzle the ginger-tamari glaze over the chicken.
9. Serve your Japanese-Inspired Glazed Chicken.

Bacon & Chicken Flatbread

Servings: 2
Cooking Time: 35 Minutes
Ingredients:

- 1 flatbread dough
- 1 chicken breast, cubed
- 100 grams breadcrumbs
- 2 eggs, beaten
- Salt and pepper to taste
- 2 teaspoons dry rosemary
- 1 teaspoon fajita seasoning
- 1 teaspoon onion powder
- 3 bacon strips
- ½ tablespoon ranch sauce

Directions:

1. Preheat your air fryer to 180°C (360°F).
2. In a mixing bowl, combine breadcrumbs, onion powder, dry rosemary, salt, and pepper.
3. Coat the cubed chicken with the breadcrumb mixture. Dip each piece of chicken into the beaten eggs and then roll them again in the dry ingredients until well coated.
4. Arrange the coated chicken pieces on one side of the greased frying basket.
5. On the other side of the basket, lay the bacon strips.
6. Air fry for 6 minutes, then turn the bacon pieces over and flip the chicken pieces. Cook for another 6 minutes until both are crispy and cooked through.
7. While the chicken and bacon are cooking, roll out the flatbread dough and spread the ranch sauce evenly over the surface.
8. Top the flatbread with the cooked bacon and chicken, and sprinkle with the fajita seasoning.
9. Close the flatbread to contain the filling and place it in the air fryer.
10. Cook for 10 minutes, flipping the flatbread once, until it becomes golden brown and crispy.
11. Let it cool for a few minutes, then slice and serve your delicious Bacon & Chicken Flatbread.

Turkey And Mushroom Burgers

Servings: 2
Cooking Time:xx
Ingredients:

- 180g mushrooms
- 500g minced turkey
- 1 tbsp of your favourite chicken seasoning, e.g. Maggi
- 1 tsp onion powder
- 1 tsp garlic powder
- Salt and pepper to taste

Directions:

1. Place the mushrooms in a food processor and puree
2. Add all the seasonings and mix well
3. Remove from the food processor and transfer to a mixing bowl
4. Add the minced turkey and combine again
5. Shape the mix into 5 burger patties
6. Spray with cooking spray and place in the air fryer
7. Cook at 160ºC for 10 minutes, until cooked.

Chicken Kiev

Servings: 4

Cooking Time:xx

Ingredients:

- 4 boneless chicken breasts
- 4 tablespoons plain/all-purpose flour (gluten-free if you wish)
- 1 egg, beaten
- 130 g/2 cups dried breadcrumbs (gluten-free if you wish, see page 9)
- GARLIC BUTTER
- 60 g/4 tablespoons salted butter, softened
- 1 large garlic clove, finely chopped

Directions:

1. Mash together the butter and garlic. Form into a sausage shape, then slice into 4 equal discs. Place in the freezer until frozen.

2. Make a deep horizontal slit across each chicken breast, taking care not to cut through to the other side. Stuff the cavity with a disc of frozen garlic butter. Place the flour in a shallow bowl, the egg in another and the breadcrumbs in a third. Coat each chicken breast first in flour, then egg, then breadcrumbs.

3. Preheat the air-fryer to 180ºC/350ºF.

4. Add the chicken Kievs to the preheated air-fryer and air-fry for 12 minutes until cooked through. This is hard to gauge as the butter inside the breast is not an indicator of doneness, so test the meat in the centre with a meat thermometer – it should be at least 75ºC/167ºF; if not, cook for another few minutes.

Cal-mex Turkey Patties

Servings: 4

Cooking Time: 30 Minutes

Ingredients:

- 40 grams crushed corn tortilla chips
- 40 grams grated American cheese
- 1 egg, beaten
- 60ml salsa
- Salt and pepper to taste
- 450 grams ground turkey
- 15ml olive oil
- 5 grams chili powder

Directions:

1. Preheat your air fryer to 165°C (330°F).

2. In a bowl, mix together the beaten egg, crushed corn tortilla chips, salsa, grated American cheese, salt, and pepper.

3. Add the ground turkey to the mixture and gently combine using your hands until just mixed.

4. Divide the meat mixture into 4 equal portions and shape them into patties about 1.25 centimeters (½ inch) thick.

5. Brush the patties with olive oil and sprinkle them with chili powder.

6. Air fry the patties for 14-16 minutes, flipping them once during cooking, until they are cooked through and golden brown.

7. Serve your Cal-Mex Turkey Patties and enjoy!

Chicken Milanese

Servings: 4

Cooking Time:xx

Ingredients:

- 130 g/1¾ cups dried breadcrumbs (gluten-free if you wish, see page 9)
- 50 g/⅔ cup grated Parmesan
- 1 teaspoon dried basil
- ½ teaspoon dried thyme
- ¼ teaspoon freshly ground black pepper
- 1 egg, beaten
- 4 tablespoons plain/all-purpose flour (gluten-free if you wish)
- 4 boneless chicken breasts

Directions:

1. Combine the breadcrumbs, cheese, herbs and pepper in a bowl. In a second bowl beat the egg, and in the third bowl have the plain/all-purpose flour. Dip each chicken breast first into the flour, then the egg, then the seasoned breadcrumbs.

2. Preheat the air-fryer to 180ºC/350ºF.

3. Add the breaded chicken breasts to the preheated air-fryer and air-fry for 12 minutes. Check the internal temperature of the chicken has reached at least 74ºC/165ºF using a meat thermometer – if not, cook for another few minutes.

Chicken Burgers With Blue Cheese Sauce

Servings: 4
Cooking Time: 40 Minutes
Ingredients:

- 60g crumbled blue cheese
- 60ml sour cream
- 30ml mayonnaise
- 15ml red hot sauce
- Salt to taste
- 45ml buffalo wing sauce
- 450g ground chicken
- 30g grated carrot
- 30g diced celery
- 1 egg white

Directions:

1. In a bowl, whisk together the blue cheese, sour cream, mayonnaise, red hot sauce, salt, and 15ml of buffalo sauce. Cover and refrigerate until ready to use.

2. Preheat your air fryer to 177°C (350°F).

3. In another bowl, combine the ground chicken, grated carrot, diced celery, egg white, and the remaining 30ml of buffalo wing sauce.

4. Form the mixture into 4 patties, making a slight indentation in the middle of each patty.

5. Place the patties in the greased air fryer basket.

6. Air fry the chicken burgers for 13 minutes or until they reach your desired doneness, flipping them once.

7. Serve the chicken burgers with the blue cheese sauce.

Sandwiches And Burgers Recipes

Best-ever Roast Beef Sandwiches

Servings: 6
Cooking Time: 30-50 Minutes
Ingredients:

- 12.5ml Olive oil
- 7.5ml Dried oregano
- 7.5ml Dried thyme
- 7.5ml Onion powder
- 7.5ml Table salt
- 7.5ml Ground black pepper
- 1.4kg Beef eye of round
- 6 Round soft rolls, such as Kaiser rolls or hamburger buns (gluten-free, if needed), split open lengthwise
- 180ml Regular, low-fat, or fat-free mayonnaise (gluten-free, if needed)
- 6 Romaine lettuce leaves, rinsed
- 6 Round tomato slices (6mm thick)

Directions:

1. Preheat the air fryer to 175°C (350°F).

2. Mix the olive oil, dried oregano, dried thyme, onion powder, salt, and black pepper in a small bowl. Spread this mixture all over the eye of round.

3. When the air fryer is at temperature, place the beef in the basket and air-fry for 30 to 50 minutes (the range depends on the size of the cut), turning the meat twice. Use an instant-read meat thermometer inserted into the thickest piece of meat to register 54°C for rare, 60°C for medium, or 65°C for well-done.

4. Use kitchen tongs to transfer the beef to a cutting board. Allow it to cool for 10 minutes.

5. If serving immediately, carve the beef into 3mm thick slices. Spread each roll with 30ml of mayonnaise and divide the beef slices between the rolls. Top with a lettuce leaf and a tomato slice and serve.

6. Alternatively, place the beef in a container, cover, and refrigerate for up to 3 days to make cold roast beef sandwiches anytime.

Black Bean Veggie Burgers

Servings: 3
Cooking Time: 10 Minutes
Ingredients:

- 225g Drained and rinsed canned black beans
- 40g Pecan pieces
- 40g Rolled oats (not quick-cooking or steel-cut; gluten-free, if needed)
- 30ml Pasteurized egg substitute (or 1 small egg), such as Egg Beaters (gluten-free, if needed)
- 10ml Red ketchup-like chili sauce, such as Heinz
- 2.5ml Ground cumin
- 2.5ml Dried oregano
- 2.5ml Table salt
- 2.5ml Ground black pepper
- Olive oil
- Olive oil spray

Directions:

1. Preheat the air fryer to 200°C (400°F).
2. Put the beans, pecans, oats, egg substitute or egg, chili sauce, cumin, oregano, salt, and pepper in a food processor. Cover and process to a coarse paste that will hold its shape like sugar-cookie dough, adding olive oil in 5ml increments to get the mixture to blend smoothly. The amount of olive oil is actually dependent on the internal moisture content of the beans and the oats. Figure on about 15ml (three 5ml additions) for the smaller batch, with proportional increases for the other batches. A little too much olive oil can't hurt, but a dry paste will fall apart as it cooks and a far-too-wet paste will stick to the basket.
3. Scrape down and remove the blade. Using clean, wet hands, form the paste into two 10cm patties for the small batch, three 10cm patties for the medium, or four 10cm patties for the large batch, setting them one by one on a cutting board.
4. Generously coat both sides of the patties with olive oil spray.
5. Set them in the basket in one layer. Air-fry undisturbed for 10 minutes, or until lightly browned and crisp at the edges.
6. Use a nonstick-safe spatula, and perhaps a flatware fork for balance, to transfer the burgers to a wire rack. Cool for 5 minutes before serving.

Asian Glazed Meatballs

Servings: 4
Cooking Time: 10 Minutes
Ingredients:

- 1 large shallot, finely chopped
- 2 cloves garlic, minced
- 1 tablespoon grated fresh ginger
- 2 teaspoons fresh thyme, finely chopped
- 225g brown mushrooms, very finely chopped (a food processor works well here)
- 30ml soy sauce
- Freshly ground black pepper
- 450g ground beef
- 225g ground pork
- 3 egg yolks
- 240ml Thai sweet chili sauce (spring roll sauce)
- 60g toasted sesame seeds
- 2 scallions, sliced

Directions:

1. Combine the shallot, garlic, ginger, thyme, mushrooms, soy sauce, freshly ground black pepper, ground beef and pork, and egg yolks in a bowl. Mix the ingredients together. Gently shape the mixture into 24 balls, about the size of a golf ball.
2. Preheat the air fryer to 190°C (380°F).
3. Working in batches, air-fry the meatballs for 8 minutes, turning the meatballs over halfway through the cooking time.
4. Drizzle some of the Thai sweet chili sauce on top of each meatball and return the basket to the air fryer. Air-fry for another 2 minutes. Reserve the remaining Thai sweet chili sauce for serving.
5. As soon as the meatballs are done, sprinkle them with toasted sesame seeds and transfer them to a serving platter.
6. Scatter the sliced scallions around and serve the meatballs warm.

Turkey Burgers

Servings: 3

Cooking Time: 23 Minutes

Ingredients:

- 500 grams Ground turkey
- 90 grams Frozen chopped spinach, thawed and squeezed dry
- 45 grams Plain panko bread crumbs (ensure they are gluten-free if needed)
- 15 grams Dijon mustard (ensure it's gluten-free if needed)
- 7.5 grams Minced garlic
- 3/4 teaspoon Table salt
- 3/4 teaspoon Ground black pepper
- Olive oil spray
- 3 Kaiser rolls (ensure they are gluten-free if needed), split open

Directions:

1. Preheat your air fryer to 190°C (375°F).

2. In a large bowl, gently combine the ground turkey, thawed and squeezed dry chopped spinach, panko bread crumbs, Dijon mustard, minced garlic, salt, and black pepper. Try to maintain some of the ground turkey's texture. Form the mixture into two 17 cm (5-inch) wide patties for a small batch, three patties for a medium batch, or four patties for a large batch.

3. Coat each side of the patties with olive oil spray.

4. Place the patties in the air fryer basket in a single layer. Air-fry without disturbing for 20 minutes or until an instant-read meat thermometer inserted into the center of a burger registers 74°C (165°F). If your air fryer is set to 180°C (360°F), you may need to add an additional 2 minutes to the cooking time.

5. Use a spatula that is safe for nonstick surfaces, and perhaps a flatware fork for balance, to transfer the burgers to a cutting board.

6. Place the split Kaiser rolls cut side down in the air fryer basket in a single layer (you may need to work in batches) and air-fry for 1 minute to lightly toast and warm them.

7. Serve the turkey burgers warm in the buns.

White Bean Veggie Burgers

Servings: 3

Cooking Time: 13 Minutes

Ingredients:

- 300 grams Drained and rinsed canned white beans
- 45 grams Rolled oats (not quick-cooking or steel-cut; ensure they are gluten-free if needed)
- 45 grams Chopped walnuts
- 10 milliliters Olive oil
- 10 milliliters Lemon juice
- 7.5 milliliters Dijon mustard (ensure it's gluten-free if needed)
- 3.75 milliliters Dried sage leaves
- 1.25 milliliters Table salt
- Olive oil spray
- 3 Whole-wheat buns or gluten-free whole-grain buns (if needed), split open

Directions:

1. Preheat your air fryer to 200°C (400°F).

2. In a food processor, combine the drained and rinsed canned white beans, rolled oats, chopped walnuts, olive oil, lemon juice, Dijon mustard, dried sage leaves, and table salt. Process until you achieve a coarse paste with a consistency similar to wet sugar-cookie dough. Make sure to stop the machine and scrape down the sides of the canister at least once during processing.

3. Scrape down and remove the blade from the food processor. With clean, wet hands, shape the bean paste into two 10.16 cm (4-inch) patties for a small batch, three patties for a medium batch, or four patties for a large batch. Generously coat each patty on both sides with olive oil spray.

4. Place the patties in the air fryer basket, leaving some space between them. Air-fry without disturbance for 12 minutes or until the patties are lightly browned and crisp at the edges. The tops of the burgers should feel firm to the touch.

5. Use a spatula that is safe for nonstick surfaces, and perhaps a flatware fork for balance, to transfer the burgers to a cutting board.

6. Place the split buns cut side down in the air fryer basket in a single layer (you may need to work in batches) and air-fry for 1 minute to lightly toast and warm them.

7. Serve the veggie burgers warm in the buns.

Chicken Apple Brie Melt

Servings: 3
Cooking Time: 13 Minutes
Ingredients:
- 3 boneless skinless chicken breasts (approximately 140-170g each)
- Vegetable oil spray
- 7.5ml Dried herbes de Provence
- 85g Brie, rind removed, thinly sliced
- 6 Thin cored apple slices
- 3 French rolls (gluten-free, if needed)
- 30ml Dijon mustard (gluten-free, if needed)

Directions:
1. Preheat the air fryer to 190°C (375°F).
2. Lightly coat all sides of the chicken breasts with vegetable oil spray. Sprinkle the breasts evenly with the herbes de Provence.
3. When the air fryer is at temperature, place the breasts in the basket and air-fry undisturbed for 10 minutes.
4. Top the chicken breasts with the apple slices, then the cheese. Air-fry undisturbed for 2 minutes, or until the cheese is melty and bubbling.
5. Use a nonstick-safe spatula and kitchen tongs, for balance, to transfer the breasts to a cutting board. Set the rolls in the basket and air-fry for 1 minute to warm through. (Putting them in the machine without splitting them keeps the insides very soft while the outside gets a little crunchy.)
6. Transfer the rolls to the cutting board. Split them open lengthwise, then spread 5ml of mustard on each cut side. Set a prepared chicken breast on the bottom of a roll and close with its top, repeating as necessary to make additional sandwiches. Serve warm.

Chicken Spiedies

Servings: 3
Cooking Time: 12 Minutes
Ingredients:
- 567 grams boneless, skinless chicken thighs, trimmed of any fat blobs and cut into 5-cm pieces
- 45 ml red wine vinegar
- 30 ml olive oil
- 30 ml minced fresh mint leaves
- 30 ml minced fresh parsley leaves
- 30 ml minced fresh dill fronds
- 2.25 ml fennel seeds
- 2.25 ml table salt
- Up to 1.25 ml red pepper flakes
- 3 long soft rolls, such as hero, hoagie, or Italian sub rolls (gluten-free, if a concern), split open lengthwise
- 67.5 ml regular or low-fat mayonnaise (not fat-free; gluten-free, if a concern)
- 22.5 ml distilled white vinegar
- 7.5 ml ground black pepper

Directions:
1. Mix the chicken, vinegar, oil, mint, parsley, dill, fennel seeds, salt, and red pepper flakes in a zip-closed plastic bag. Seal, gently massage the marinade ingredients into the meat, and refrigerate for at least 2 hours or up to 6 hours. (Longer than that and the meat can turn rubbery.)
2. Set the plastic bag out on the counter (to make the contents a little less frigid). Preheat the air fryer to 200°C (400°F).
3. When the machine is at temperature, use kitchen tongs to set the chicken thighs in the basket (discard any remaining marinade) and air-fry undisturbed for 6 minutes. Turn the thighs over and continue air-frying undisturbed for 6 minutes more, until well browned, cooked through, and even a little crunchy.
4. Dump the contents of the basket onto a wire rack and cool for 2 or 3 minutes. Divide the chicken evenly between the rolls.
5. Whisk the mayonnaise, vinegar, and black pepper in a small bowl until smooth. Drizzle this sauce over the chicken pieces in the rolls.

Thai-style Pork Sliders

Servings: 4
Cooking Time: 15 Minutes
Ingredients:
- 315 grams Ground pork
- 2½ tablespoons Very thinly sliced scallions, white and green parts
- 4 teaspoons Minced peeled fresh ginger
- 2½ teaspoons Fish sauce (ensure it's gluten-free if needed)
- 2 teaspoons Thai curry paste (check for gluten-free certification if needed)
- 2 teaspoons Light brown sugar
- ¾ teaspoon Ground black pepper
- 4 Slider buns (ensure they are gluten-free if needed)

Directions:

1. Preheat your air fryer to 190°C (375°F).

2. In a bowl, gently combine the ground pork, scallions, minced ginger, fish sauce, Thai curry paste, light brown sugar, and ground black pepper until well mixed.

3. With clean, wet hands, shape about ⅓ cup of the pork mixture into a slider approximately 6.35 cm (2.5 inches) in diameter. Repeat this process until you've used up all the pork mixture. For a small batch, make 3 sliders, for a medium batch, make 4 sliders, and for a large batch, make 6 sliders. Keep wetting your hands to help the patties hold together.

4. Once the air fryer reaches the desired temperature, place the sliders in the basket in a single layer. Air-fry without disturbing for 14 minutes, or until the sliders turn golden brown, have caramelized edges, and an instant-read meat thermometer inserted into the center of a slider reads 71°C (160°F).

5. Use a spatula that is safe for nonstick surfaces, and perhaps a flatware fork for balance, to transfer the sliders to a cutting board.

6. Place the slider buns cut side down in the air fryer basket in a single layer (you may need to work in batches) and air-fry for 1 minute without disturbance to lightly toast and warm them.

7. Serve the warm Thai-Style Pork Sliders in the buns.

Perfect Burgers

Servings: 3
Cooking Time: 13 Minutes

Ingredients:

- 530 grams 90% lean ground beef
- 22.5 milliliters Worcestershire sauce (gluten-free, if a concern)
- 2.5 grams Ground black pepper
- 3 Hamburger buns (gluten-free if a concern), split open

Directions:

1. Preheat the air fryer to 190°C (375°F).

2. Gently mix the ground beef, Worcestershire sauce, and pepper in a bowl until well combined but preserving as much of the meat's fibers as possible. Divide this mixture into two 17 cm (5-inch) patties for the small batch, three 12.7 cm (5-inch) patties for the medium, or four 12.7 cm (5-inch) patties for the large. Make a thumbprint indentation in the center of each patty, about halfway through the meat.

3. Set the patties in the basket in one layer with some space between them. Air-fry undisturbed for 10 minutes, or until an instant-read meat thermometer inserted into the center of a burger registers 71°C (160°F) (a medium-well burger). You may need to add 2 minutes of cooking time if the air fryer is at 182°C (360°F).

4. Use a nonstick-safe spatula, and perhaps a flatware fork for balance, to transfer the burgers to a cutting board. Set the buns cut side down in the basket in one layer (working in batches as necessary) and air-fry undisturbed for 1 minute, to toast a bit and warm up. Serve the burgers in the warm buns.

Dijon Thyme Burgers

Servings: 3
Cooking Time: 18 Minutes

Ingredients:

- 450 grams lean ground beef
- 30 grams panko breadcrumbs
- 25 grams finely chopped onion
- 45 milliliters Dijon mustard
- 15 milliliters chopped fresh thyme
- 20 milliliters Worcestershire sauce
- 5 grams salt
- Freshly ground black pepper
- Topping (optional):
- 30 milliliters Dijon mustard
- 15 grams dark brown sugar
- 5 milliliters Worcestershire sauce
- 115 grams sliced Swiss cheese, optional

Directions:

1. Combine all the burger ingredients together in a large bowl and mix well. Divide the meat into 4 equal portions and then form the burgers, being careful not to over-handle the meat. One good way to do this is to throw the meat back and forth from one hand to another, packing the meat each time you catch it. Flatten the balls into patties, making an indentation in the center of each patty with your thumb (this will help it stay flat as it cooks) and flattening the sides of the burgers so that they will fit nicely into the air fryer basket.

2. Preheat the air fryer to 190°C (370°F).

3. If you don't have room for all four burgers, air-fry two or three burgers at a time for 8 minutes. Flip the burgers over and air-fry for another 6 minutes.

4. While the burgers are cooking, combine the Dijon mustard, dark brown sugar, and Worcestershire sauce in a small bowl and mix well. This optional topping for the burgers adds a boost of flavor at the end. Spread the Dijon topping evenly on each burger. If you cooked the burgers in batches, return the first batch to the cooker at this time – it's ok to place the fourth burger on top of the others in the center of the basket. Air-fry the burgers for another 3 minutes.

5. Finally, if desired, top each burger with a slice of Swiss cheese. Lower the air fryer temperature to 165°C (330°F) and air-fry for another minute to melt the cheese. Serve the burgers on toasted brioche buns, dressed the way you like them.

Thanksgiving Turkey Sandwiches

Servings: 3
Cooking Time: 10 Minutes
Ingredients:
- 135 grams Herb-seasoned stuffing mix (not cornbread-style; ensure it's gluten-free if needed)
- 1 Large egg white
- 2 tablespoons Water
- 3 Turkey breast cutlets, about 140-170 grams each
- Vegetable oil spray
- 67.5 grams Purchased cranberry sauce, preferably whole berry
- 1/8 teaspoon Ground cinnamon
- 1/8 teaspoon Ground dried ginger
- 67.5 grams Regular, low-fat, or fat-free mayonnaise (ensure it's gluten-free if needed)
- 90 grams Shredded Brussels sprouts
- 3 Kaiser rolls (ensure they are gluten-free if needed), split open

Directions:
1. Preheat your air fryer to 190°C (375°F).
2. Place the herb-seasoned stuffing mix in a heavy zip-closed bag, seal it, and lay it flat on your counter. Roll a rolling pin over the bag to crush the stuffing mix to a rough sand-like consistency. Alternatively, you can pulse the stuffing mix in a food processor until you achieve the desired texture.
3. Set up two shallow soup plates or small pie plates on your counter. In one, whisk the egg white with water until foamy. In the other, place the ground stuffing mix.

4. Dip each turkey cutlet in the egg white mixture, coating both sides and allowing any excess egg white to drip back into the bowl. Then, coat the cutlet evenly on both sides with the ground stuffing mix, pressing gently to ensure it adheres well. Lightly coat each cutlet on both sides with vegetable oil spray.

5. Place the coated cutlets in the air fryer basket in a single layer. Air-fry without disturbing for 10 minutes or until they are crisp and browned. Use kitchen tongs to transfer the cutlets to a wire rack to cool for a few minutes.

6. While the cutlets are cooling, mix the cranberry sauce with the ground cinnamon and ginger in a small bowl. In a separate bowl, combine the shredded Brussels sprouts and mayonnaise, ensuring the vegetables are evenly coated.

7. Assemble the sandwiches by spreading about 1½ tablespoons of the cranberry mixture on the cut side of the bottom half of each Kaiser roll. Place a turkey cutlet on top, then spread approximately 3 tablespoons of the Brussels sprouts mixture evenly over the cutlet. Finish by placing the other half of the roll on top.

Chicken Club Sandwiches

Servings: 3
Cooking Time: 15 Minutes
Ingredients:
- 3 boneless skinless chicken breasts (approximately 140-170g each)
- 6 Thick-cut bacon strips (gluten-free, if needed)
- 3 Long soft rolls, such as hero, hoagie, or Italian sub rolls (gluten-free, if needed)
- 3 tablespoons Regular, low-fat, or fat-free mayonnaise (gluten-free, if needed)
- 3 Lettuce leaves, preferably romaine or iceberg
- 6 6mm-thick tomato slices

Directions:
1. Preheat the air fryer to 190°C (375°F).
2. Wrap each chicken breast with 2 strips of bacon, spiraling the bacon around the meat, slightly overlapping the strips on each revolution. Start the second strip of bacon farther down the breast but on a line with the start of the first strip so they both end at a lined-up point on the chicken breast.
3. When the air fryer is at temperature, set the wrapped breasts bacon-seam side down in the basket with space between them. Air-fry undisturbed for 12 minutes, until

the bacon is browned, crisp, and cooked through, and an instant-read meat thermometer inserted into the center of a breast registers 74°C (165°F). You may need to add 2 minutes in the air fryer if the temperature is at 180°C (360°F).

4. Use kitchen tongs to transfer the breasts to a wire rack. Split the rolls open lengthwise and set them cut side down in the basket. Air-fry for 1 minute, or until warmed through.

5. Use kitchen tongs to transfer the rolls to a cutting board. Spread 15ml mayonnaise on the cut side of one half of each roll. Top with a chicken breast, lettuce leaf, and tomato slice. Serve warm.

Sausage And Pepper Subs

Servings: 3
Cooking Time: 11 Minutes
Ingredients:
- 3 Sweet Italian sausages (approximately 255 grams total) (ensure they are gluten-free if needed)
- 1½ Medium red or green bell peppers, deseeded and cut into 1.25 cm wide strips
- 1 medium Yellow or white onion, peeled, halved, and thinly sliced into half-moons
- 3 Long soft rolls, like sub rolls or baguettes (ensure they are gluten-free if needed), split open lengthwise
- Balsamic vinegar, for garnish
- Fresh basil leaves, for garnish
- Instructions:
- Preheat your air fryer to 200°C (400°F).
- Once the air fryer reaches the desired temperature, place the sausage links in the basket in a single layer. Air-fry without disturbance for 5 minutes.
- Add the pepper strips and onions to the air fryer. Continue air-frying, tossing and rearranging them every minute for 5 minutes, or until the sausages are browned and an instant-read meat thermometer inserted into one of the sausages registers 71°C (160°F).
- Use a spatula that is safe for nonstick surfaces and kitchen tongs to transfer the sausages and vegetables to a cutting board.
- Place the rolls cut side down in the air fryer basket in a single layer (you may need to work in batches) and air-fry for 1 minute without disturbance to lightly toast and warm them.

- Place one sausage along with some pepper strips and onions into each warmed roll. Drizzle a bit of balsamic vinegar over the sandwich fillings and garnish with fresh basil leaves.

Inside-out Cheeseburgers

Servings: 3
Cooking Time: 9-11 Minutes
Ingredients:
- 510 grams lean ground beef (90% lean)
- ¾ teaspoon dried oregano
- ¾ teaspoon table salt
- ¾ teaspoon ground black pepper
- ¼ teaspoon garlic powder
- 45 grams (about 40g) shredded Cheddar, Swiss, or other semi-firm cheese, or a purchased blend of shredded cheeses
- 3 hamburger buns (gluten-free, if a concern), split open
Directions:
1. Preheat the air fryer to 190°C (375°F).
2. Gently mix the ground beef, oregano, salt, pepper, and garlic powder in a bowl until well combined without turning the mixture to mush. Form it into two 6-inch patties for the small batch, three for the medium, or four for the large.
3. Place 2 tablespoons of the shredded cheese in the center of each patty. With clean hands, fold the sides of the patty up to cover the cheese, then pick it up and roll it gently into a ball to seal the cheese inside. Gently press it back into a 5-inch burger without letting any cheese squish out. Continue filling and preparing more burgers, as needed.
4. Place the burgers in the basket in one layer and air-fry undisturbed for 8 minutes for medium or 10 minutes for well-done. (An instant-read meat thermometer won't work for these burgers because it will hit the mostly melted cheese inside and offer a hotter temperature than the surrounding meat.)
5. Use a nonstick-safe spatula, and perhaps a flatware fork for balance, to transfer the burgers to a cutting board. Set the buns cut side down in the basket in one layer (working in batches as necessary) and air-fry undisturbed for 1 minute, to toast a bit and warm up. Cool the burgers a few minutes more, then serve them warm in the buns.

Provolone Stuffed Meatballs

Servings: 4
Cooking Time: 12 Minutes
Ingredients:

- 15 milliliters olive oil
- 1 small onion, very finely chopped
- 1 to 2 cloves garlic, minced
- 340 grams ground beef
- 340 grams ground pork
- 180 milliliters breadcrumbs
- 60 grams grated Parmesan cheese
- 60 milliliters finely chopped fresh parsley (or 15 milliliters dried parsley)
- 2.5 milliliters dried oregano
- 7.5 milliliters salt
- freshly ground black pepper
- 2 eggs, lightly beaten
- 142 grams sharp or aged provolone cheese, cut into 2.5-centimeter (1-inch) cubes

Directions:

1. Preheat a skillet over medium-high heat. Add the oil and cook the onion and garlic until tender, but not browned.
2. Transfer the onion and garlic to a large bowl and add the beef, pork, breadcrumbs, Parmesan cheese, parsley, oregano, salt, pepper, and eggs. Mix well until all the ingredients are combined.
3. Divide the mixture into 12 evenly sized balls. Make one meatball at a time by pressing a hole in the meatball mixture with your finger and pushing a piece of provolone cheese into the hole. Mold the meat back into a ball, enclosing the cheese.
4. Preheat the air fryer to 193°C (380°F).
5. Working in two batches, transfer six of the meatballs to the air fryer basket and air-fry for 12 minutes, shaking the basket and turning the meatballs a couple of times during the cooking process. Repeat with the remaining six meatballs. You can pop the first batch of meatballs into the air fryer for the last two minutes of cooking to re-heat them. Serve warm.

Chicken Gyros

Servings: 4
Cooking Time: 14 Minutes
Ingredients:

- 4 boneless skinless chicken thighs (approximately 110-140g each), trimmed of any fat blobs
- 30ml Lemon juice
- 30ml Red wine vinegar
- 30ml Olive oil
- 10g Dried oregano
- 10g Minced garlic
- 5g Table salt
- 5g Ground black pepper
- 4 Pita pockets (gluten-free, if needed)
- 120g Chopped tomatoes
- 120ml Bottled regular, low-fat, or fat-free ranch dressing (gluten-free, if needed)

Directions:

1. Mix the thighs, lemon juice, vinegar, oil, oregano, garlic, salt, and pepper in a zip-closed bag. Seal the bag, gently massage the marinade into the meat through the plastic, and refrigerate for at least 2 hours or up to 6 hours. (Marinating longer can result in rubbery meat.)
2. Set the plastic bag out on the counter (to make the contents a little less cold). Preheat the air fryer to 190°C (375°F).
3. When the air fryer reaches temperature, use kitchen tongs to place the thighs in the basket in a single layer. Discard the marinade. Air-fry the chicken thighs undisturbed for 12 minutes, or until browned and an instant-read meat thermometer inserted into the thickest part of one thigh registers 74°C (165°F). You may need to air-fry the chicken for an additional 2 minutes if the air fryer's temperature is at 180°C (360°F).
4. Use kitchen tongs to transfer the thighs to a cutting board. Let them cool for 5 minutes, then place one thigh in each of the pita pockets. Top each with 30g chopped tomatoes and 30ml dressing. Serve warm.

Philly Cheesesteak Sandwiches

Servings: 3
Cooking Time: 9 Minutes
Ingredients:

- 340 grams Shaved beef
- 15 milliliters Worcestershire sauce (gluten-free, if a concern)
- 1.25 grams Garlic powder
- 0.6 grams Mild paprika
- 45 grams Frozen bell pepper strips (do not thaw)

- 34 grams Very thin yellow or white medium onion slice(s)
- 170 grams (6 to 8 slices) Provolone cheese slices
- 3 Long soft rolls such as hero, hoagie, or Italian sub rolls, or hot dog buns (gluten-free, if a concern), split open lengthwise

Directions:

1. Preheat the air fryer to 200°C (400°F).
2. When the machine is at temperature, spread the shaved beef in the basket, leaving a 1.3 cm (½-inch) perimeter around the meat for good air flow. Sprinkle the meat with the Worcestershire sauce, paprika, and garlic powder. Spread the peppers and onions on top of the meat.
3. Air-fry undisturbed for 6 minutes, or until cooked through. Set the cheese on top of the meat. Continue air-frying undisturbed for 3 minutes, or until the cheese has melted.
4. Use kitchen tongs to divide the meat and cheese layers in the basket between the rolls or buns. Serve hot.

Eggplant Parmesan Subs

Servings: 2
Cooking Time: 13 Minutes

Ingredients:

- 4 Peeled eggplant slices (about 1.25 cm thick and 7.5 cm in diameter)
- Olive oil spray
- 2 tablespoons plus 2 teaspoons Jarred pizza sauce, any variety except creamy
- 25 grams Finely grated Parmesan cheese
- 2 Small, long soft rolls, such as hero, hoagie, or Italian sub rolls (gluten-free, if a concern), split open lengthwise

Directions:

1. Preheat the air fryer to 175°C (350°F).
2. When the machine is at temperature, coat both sides of the eggplant slices with olive oil spray. Set them in the basket in one layer and air-fry undisturbed for 10 minutes, until lightly browned and softened.
3. Increase the machine's temperature to 190°C (375°F) (or 190°C, if that's the closest setting—unless the machine is already at 180°C, in which case leave it alone). Top each eggplant slice with 2 teaspoons pizza sauce, then 1 tablespoon cheese. Air-fry undisturbed for 2 minutes, or until the cheese has melted.
4. Use a nonstick-safe spatula, and perhaps a flatware fork for balance, to transfer the eggplant slices cheese

side up to a cutting board. Set the roll(s) cut side down in the basket in one layer (working in batches as necessary) and air-fry undisturbed for 1 minute, to toast the rolls a bit and warm them up. Set 2 eggplant slices in each warm roll.

Reuben Sandwiches

Servings: 2
Cooking Time: 11 Minutes

Ingredients:

- 227 grams Sliced deli corned beef
- 20 milliliters Regular or low-fat mayonnaise (not fat-free)
- 4 Rye bread slices
- 30 milliliters Russian dressing
- 120 milliliters Purchased sauerkraut, squeezed by the handful over the sink to get rid of excess moisture
- 56 grams (2 to 4 slices) Swiss cheese slices (optional)

Directions:

1. Set the corned beef in the basket, slip the basket into the air fryer, and heat it to 204°C (400°F). Air-fry undisturbed for 3 minutes from the time the basket is put in the machine, just to warm up the meat.
2. Use kitchen tongs to transfer the corned beef to a cutting board. Spread 5 milliliters (1 teaspoon) mayonnaise on one side of each slice of rye bread, rubbing the mayonnaise into the bread with a small flatware knife.
3. Place the bread slices mayonnaise side down on a cutting board. Spread the Russian dressing over the "dry" side of each slice. For one sandwich, top one slice of bread with the corned beef, sauerkraut, and cheese (if using). For two sandwiches, top two slices of bread each with half of the corned beef, sauerkraut, and cheese (if using). Close the sandwiches with the remaining bread, setting it mayonnaise side up on top.
4. Set the sandwich(es) in the basket and air-fry undisturbed for 8 minutes, or until browned and crunchy.
5. Use a nonstick-safe spatula, and perhaps a flatware fork for balance, to transfer the sandwich(es) to a cutting board. Cool for 2 or 3 minutes before slicing in half and serving.

Inside Out Cheeseburgers

Servings: 2
Cooking Time: 20 Minutes
Ingredients:
- 340 grams lean ground beef
- 3 tablespoons minced onion
- 4 teaspoons ketchup
- 2 teaspoons yellow mustard
- Salt and freshly ground black pepper
- 4 slices of Cheddar cheese, broken into smaller pieces
- 8 hamburger dill pickle chips

Directions:
1. Combine the ground beef, minced onion, ketchup, mustard, salt, and pepper in a large bowl. Mix well to thoroughly combine the ingredients. Divide the meat into four equal portions.
2. To make the stuffed burgers, flatten each portion of meat into a thin patty. Place 4 pickle chips and half of the cheese onto the center of two of the patties, leaving a rim around the edge of the patty exposed. Place the remaining two patties on top of the first and press the meat together firmly, sealing the edges tightly. With the burgers on a flat surface, press the sides of the burger with the palm of your hand to create a straight edge. This will help keep the stuffing inside the burger while it cooks.
3. Preheat the air fryer to 190°C (370°F).
4. Place the burgers inside the air fryer basket and air-fry for 20 minutes, flipping the burgers over halfway through the cooking time.
5. Serve the cheeseburgers on buns with lettuce and tomato.

Mexican Cheeseburgers

Servings: 4
Cooking Time: 22 Minutes
Ingredients:
- 567 grams ground beef
- 60 grams finely chopped onion
- 60 grams crushed yellow corn tortilla chips
- 35 grams (1.25-ounce) packet taco seasoning
- 60 grams canned diced green chilies
- 1 egg, lightly beaten
- 113 grams pepper jack cheese, grated
- 4 (12-inch) flour tortillas
- shredded lettuce, sour cream, guacamole, salsa (for topping)

Directions:
1. Combine the ground beef, minced onion, crushed tortilla chips, taco seasoning, green chilies, and egg in a large bowl. Mix thoroughly until combined – your hands are good tools for this. Divide the meat into four equal portions and shape each portion into an oval-shaped burger.
2. Preheat the air fryer to 188°C (370°F).
3. Air-fry the burgers for 18 minutes, turning them over halfway through the cooking time. Divide the cheese between the burgers, lower fryer to 171°C (340°F), and air-fry for an additional 4 minutes to melt the cheese. (This will give you a burger that is medium-well. If you prefer your cheeseburger medium-rare, shorten the cooking time to about 15 minutes and then add the cheese and proceed with the recipe.)
4. While the burgers are cooking, warm the tortillas wrapped in aluminum foil in a 176°C (350°F) oven or in a skillet with a little oil over medium-high heat for a couple of minutes. Keep the tortillas warm until the burgers are ready.
5. To assemble the burgers, spread sour cream over three-quarters of the tortillas and top each with some shredded lettuce and salsa. Place the Mexican cheeseburgers on the lettuce and top with guacamole. Fold the tortillas around the burger, starting with the bottom and then folding the sides in over the top. (A little sour cream can help hold the seam of the tortilla together.) Serve immediately.

Salmon Burgers

Servings: 3
Cooking Time: 8 Minutes
Ingredients:
- 510 grams Skinless salmon fillet, preferably fattier Atlantic salmon
- 22.5 milliliters Minced chives or the green part of a scallion
- 120 milliliters Plain panko bread crumbs (gluten-free, if a concern)
- 7.5 milliliters Dijon mustard (gluten-free, if a concern)
- 7.5 milliliters Drained and rinsed capers, minced
- 7.5 milliliters Lemon juice
- 1.25 milliliters Table salt
- 1.25 milliliters Ground black pepper

- Vegetable oil spray

Directions:

1. Preheat the air fryer to 190°C (375°F).

2. Cut the salmon into pieces that will fit in a food processor. Cover and pulse until coarsely chopped. Add the chives and pulse to combine, until the fish is ground but not a paste. Scrape down and remove the blade. Scrape the salmon mixture into a bowl. Add the bread crumbs, mustard, capers, lemon juice, salt, and pepper. Stir gently until well combined.

3. Use clean and dry hands to form the mixture into two 5-inch patties for a small batch, three 5-inch patties for a medium batch, or four 5-inch patties for a large one.

4. Coat both sides of each patty with vegetable oil spray. Set them in the basket in one layer and air-fry undisturbed for 8 minutes, or until browned and an instant-read meat thermometer inserted into the center of a burger registers 63°C (145°F).

5. Use a nonstick-safe spatula, and perhaps a flatware fork for balance, to transfer the burgers to a wire rack. Cool for 2 or 3 minutes before serving.

Crunchy Falafel Balls

Servings: 8
Cooking Time: 16 Minutes

Ingredients:

- 590 ml Drained and rinsed canned chickpeas
- 60 ml Olive oil
- 45 ml All-purpose flour
- 7.5 ml Dried oregano
- 7.5 ml Dried sage leaves
- 7.5 ml Dried thyme
- 3.75 ml Table salt
- Olive oil spray

Directions:

1. Preheat the air fryer to 200°C (400°F).

2. Place the chickpeas, olive oil, flour, oregano, sage, thyme, and salt in a food processor. Cover and process into a paste, stopping the machine at least once to scrape down the inside of the canister.

3. Scrape down and remove the blade. Using clean, wet hands, form 30 ml (2 tablespoons) of the paste into a ball, then continue making 9 more balls for a small batch, 15 more for a medium one, and 19 more for a large batch. Generously coat the balls in olive oil spray.

4. Set the balls in the basket in one layer with a little space between them and air-fry undisturbed for 16 minutes, or until well browned and crisp.

5. Dump the contents of the basket onto a wire rack. Cool for 5 minutes before serving.

Chicken Saltimbocca Sandwiches

Servings: 3
Cooking Time: 11 Minutes

Ingredients:

- 3 boneless, skinless chicken breasts (about 150-180g each)
- 6 thin prosciutto slices
- 6 provolone cheese slices
- 3 long soft rolls, such as hero, hoagie, or Italian sub rolls (gluten-free, if needed), split open lengthwise
- 3 tablespoons pesto, purchased or homemade (see the headnote)

Directions:

1. Preheat the air fryer to 200°C (400°F).

2. Wrap each chicken breast with 2 prosciutto slices, spiraling the prosciutto around the breast and overlapping the slices a bit to cover the breast. The prosciutto will stick to the chicken more readily than bacon does.

3. When the machine is at temperature, set the wrapped chicken breasts in the basket and air-fry undisturbed for 10 minutes, or until the prosciutto is frizzled and the chicken is cooked through.

4. Overlap 2 cheese slices on each breast. Air-fry undisturbed for 1 minute, or until melted. Take the basket out of the machine.

5. Smear the insides of the rolls with the pesto, then use kitchen tongs to put a wrapped and cheesy chicken breast in each roll.

Chili Cheese Dogs

Servings: 3
Cooking Time: 12 Minutes
Ingredients:

- 340 grams lean ground beef
- 22.5 ml chile powder
- 240 ml plus 30 ml jarred sofrito
- 3 Hot dogs (gluten-free, if a concern)
- 3 Hot dog buns (gluten-free, if a concern), split open lengthwise
- 45 ml finely chopped scallion
- 270 ml (a little more than 57 grams) Shredded Cheddar cheese

Directions:

1. Crumble the ground beef into a medium or large saucepan set over medium heat. Brown well, stirring often to break up the clumps. Add the chile powder and cook for 30 seconds, stirring the whole time. Stir in the sofrito and bring to a simmer. Reduce the heat to low and simmer, stirring occasionally, for 5 minutes. Keep warm.

2. Preheat the air fryer to 200°C (400°F).

3. When the machine is at temperature, put the hot dogs in the basket and air-fry undisturbed for 10 minutes, or until the hot dogs are bubbling and blistered, even a little crisp.

4. Use kitchen tongs to put the hot dogs in the buns. Top each with 150 ml of the ground beef mixture, 15 ml of the minced scallion, and 90 ml of the cheese. (The scallion should go under the cheese so it superheats and wilts a bit.) Set the filled hot dog buns in the basket and air-fry undisturbed for 2 minutes, or until the cheese has melted.

5. Remove the basket from the machine. Cool the chili cheese dogs in the basket for 5 minutes before serving.

Desserts And Sweets Recipes

Baked Apple Crisp

Servings: 4
Cooking Time: 23 Minutes
Ingredients:

- 2 large Granny Smith apples, peeled, cored, and chopped
- 60g granulated sugar
- 60g plus 2 teaspoons flour, divided
- 2 teaspoons milk
- 1/4 teaspoon cinnamon
- 30g oats
- 60g brown sugar
- 2 tablespoons unsalted butter
- 1/8 teaspoon baking powder
- 1/8 teaspoon salt

Directions:

1. Preheat the air fryer to 175°C (350°F).

2. In a medium bowl, mix the apples, the granulated sugar, 2 teaspoons of flour, the milk, and the cinnamon.

3. Spray 4 oven-safe ramekins with cooking spray. Divide the filling among the four ramekins.

4. In a small bowl, mix the oats, the brown sugar, the remaining 60g of flour, the butter, the baking powder, and the salt. Use your fingers or a pastry blender to crumble the butter into pea-size pieces.

5. Divide the topping over the top of the apple filling. Cover the apple crisps with foil.

6. Place the covered apple crisps in the air fryer basket and cook for 20 minutes.

7. Uncover and continue cooking for 3 minutes or until the surface is golden and crunchy.

Blueberry Crisp

Servings: 6
Cooking Time: 13 Minutes
Ingredients:

- 450 grams fresh or thawed frozen blueberries
- 80 grams granulated white sugar
- 15 grams instant tapioca
- 40 grams all-purpose flour
- 40 grams rolled oats (not quick-cooking or steel-cut)
- 40 grams chopped walnuts or pecans
- 40 grams packed light brown sugar
- 75 grams plus 1 teaspoon (85 grams total) butter, melted and cooled
- 1.5 grams ground cinnamon
- 1 gram table salt

Directions:

1. Preheat the air fryer to 200°C (400°F).
2. Mix the blueberries, granulated white sugar, and instant tapioca in a 6-inch round cake pan for a small batch, a 7-inch round cake pan for a medium batch, or an 8-inch round cake pan for a large batch.
3. Once the air fryer has reached the desired temperature, place the cake pan in the basket and air-fry undisturbed for 5 minutes or until the blueberries begin to bubble.
4. While the blueberries are cooking, mix the flour, oats, nuts, brown sugar, melted butter, ground cinnamon, and salt in a medium bowl until well combined.
5. After the blueberries have started to bubble, evenly crumble the flour mixture on top. Continue air-frying undisturbed for 8 minutes, or until the topping has browned slightly and the filling is bubbling.
6. Use two hot pads or silicone baking mitts to transfer the cake pan to a wire rack. Allow it to cool for at least 10 minutes or until it reaches room temperature before serving.

Mini Carrot Cakes

Servings: 6
Cooking Time: 25 Minutes
Ingredients:

- 240ml grated carrots
- 60ml raw honey
- 60ml olive oil
- 2.5ml vanilla extract
- 2.5ml lemon zest
- 1 egg
- 60ml unsweetened applesauce
- 160g plain flour
- 3.75ml baking powder
- 2.5ml baking soda
- 2.5ml ground cinnamon
- 1.25ml ground nutmeg
- 0.625ml ground ginger
- A pinch of salt
- 60g chopped hazelnuts
- 30ml chopped sultanas

Directions:

1. Preheat the air fryer to 190°C (380°F).
2. In a bowl, combine the grated carrots, raw honey, olive oil, vanilla extract, lemon zest, egg, and applesauce.
3. In a separate bowl, sift the plain flour, baking powder, baking soda, ground cinnamon, ground nutmeg, ground ginger, and a pinch of salt.
4. Add the wet ingredients to the dry ingredients and mix until just combined.
5. Fold in the chopped hazelnuts and sultanas.
6. Grease muffin cups and fill them three-quarters full with the batter.
7. Place the filled muffin cups in the air fryer's frying basket.
8. Bake for 10-12 minutes until a toothpick inserted into the center of a cupcake comes out clean.
9. Serve and enjoy your Mini Carrot Cakes!

Chewy Coconut Cake

Servings: 6
Cooking Time: 18-22 Minutes
Ingredients:

- 100 grams plus 2.5 tablespoons All-purpose flour
- 3/4 teaspoon Baking powder
- 1/8 teaspoon Table salt
- 85 grams (1 stick minus 1/2 tablespoon) Butter, at room temperature
- 85 grams plus 1 tablespoon Granulated white sugar
- 75 grams Packed light brown sugar
- 75 grams Pasteurized egg substitute, such as Egg Beaters
- 10 milliliters Vanilla extract
- 40 grams Unsweetened shredded coconut
- Baking spray

Directions:

1. Preheat the air fryer to 160°C (or 165°C if that's the closest setting).

2. Mix the flour, baking powder, and salt in a small bowl until well combined.

3. Using an electric hand mixer at medium speed, beat the butter, granulated white sugar, and brown sugar in a medium bowl until creamy and smooth, about 3 minutes, occasionally scraping down the inside of the bowl. Beat in the egg substitute or egg and vanilla until smooth.

4. Scrape down and remove the beaters. Fold in the flour mixture with a rubber spatula just until all the flour is moistened. Fold in the coconut until the mixture is a uniform color.

5. Use the baking spray to generously coat the inside of a 15 cm (6-inch) round cake pan for a small batch, an 18 cm (7-inch) round cake pan for a medium batch, or a 20 cm (8-inch) round cake pan for a large batch. Scrape and spread the batter into the pan, smoothing the batter out to an even layer.

6. Set the pan in the basket and air-fry for 18 minutes for a 15 cm (6-inch) layer, 20 minutes for an 18 cm (7-inch) layer, or 22 minutes for a 20 cm (8-inch) layer, or until the cake is well browned and set even if there's a little soft give right at the center. Start checking it at the 16-minute mark to know where you are.

7. Use hot pads or silicone baking mitts to transfer the cake pan to a wire rack. Cool for at least 1 hour or up to 4 hours. Use a nonstick-safe knife to slice the cake into wedges right in the pan, lifting them out one by one.

8. Enjoy your Chewy Coconut Cake!

Fried Twinkies

Servings: 6
Cooking Time: 5 Minutes
Ingredients:

- 2 Large egg white(s)
- 2 tablespoons Water
- 255 grams (about 9 ounces) Ground gingersnap cookie crumbs
- 6 Twinkies
- Vegetable oil spray

Directions:

1. Preheat your air fryer to 200°C (400°F).

2. Set up and fill two shallow soup plates or small pie plates on your counter: one for the egg white(s), whisked with the water until foamy, and one for the gingersnap crumbs.

3. Dip a Twinkie in the egg white(s), turning it to coat on all sides, including the ends. Allow any excess egg white mixture to drip back into the bowl, then place the Twinkie in the crumbs. Roll it to coat on all sides, including the ends, pressing gently to ensure an even coating. Repeat this process for each Twinkie: dip in egg white(s) followed by the crumbs. Lightly coat each prepared Twinkie on all sides with vegetable oil spray. Set them aside and repeat the double-dipping and spraying process for the remaining Twinkies.

4. Place the Twinkies flat side up in the air fryer basket, ensuring there is enough space between them for air circulation. Air-fry for 5 minutes, or until they are browned and crunchy.

5. Use a nonstick-safe spatula to gently transfer the Twinkies to a wire rack. Allow them to cool for at least 10 minutes before serving.

Annie's Chocolate Chunk Hazelnut Cookies

Servings: 24
Cooking Time: 12 Minutes
Ingredients:

- 225g butter, softened
- 200g brown sugar
- 100g granulated sugar
- 2 eggs, lightly beaten
- 1½ teaspoons vanilla extract
- 190g all-purpose flour
- 50g rolled oats
- 1 teaspoon baking soda
- ½ teaspoon salt
- 360g chocolate chunks
- 65g toasted chopped hazelnuts

Directions:

1. Cream the butter and sugars together until light and fluffy using a stand mixer or electric hand mixer. Add the eggs and vanilla, and beat until well combined.

2. Combine the flour, rolled oats, baking soda, and salt in a second bowl. Gradually add the dry ingredients to the wet ingredients with a wooden spoon or spatula. Stir in the chocolate chunks and hazelnuts until distributed throughout the dough.

3. Shape the cookies into small balls about the size of golf balls and place them on a baking sheet. Freeze the cookie balls for at least 30 minutes, or package them in as airtight a package as you can and keep them in your freezer.

4. When you're ready for a delicious snack or dessert, preheat the air fryer to 175°C (350°F). Cut a piece of parchment paper to fit the number of cookies you are baking. Place the parchment down in the air fryer basket and place the frozen cookie ball or balls on top (remember to leave room for them to expand).

5. Air-fry the cookies at 175°C (350°F) for 12 minutes, or until they are done to your liking. Let them cool for a few minutes before enjoying your freshly baked cookie.

Honey-roasted Mixed Nuts

Servings: 8
Cooking Time: 15 Minutes
Ingredients:

- 60 grams raw, shelled pistachios
- 60 grams raw almonds
- 125 grams raw walnuts
- 30 milliliters filtered water
- 30 milliliters honey
- 15 milliliters vegetable oil
- 30 grams sugar
- 1/2 teaspoon salt

Directions:

1. Preheat the air fryer to 150°C (300°F).

2. Lightly spray an air-fryer-safe pan with olive oil. Place the pistachios, almonds, and walnuts inside the pan, and then place the pan inside the air fryer basket.

3. Cook for 15 minutes, shaking the basket every 5 minutes to rotate the nuts for even roasting.

4. While the nuts are roasting, in a small pan, boil the water and stir in the honey and oil. Continue to stir while cooking until the water begins to evaporate, and a thick syrup is formed. The syrup should stick to the back of a wooden spoon when mixed. Turn off the heat.

5. Remove the nuts from the air fryer when cooking is completed, and spoon them into the stovetop pan with the honey syrup. Use a spatula to coat the nuts with the honey syrup.

6. Line a baking sheet with parchment paper and spoon the coated nuts onto the sheet.

7. Lightly sprinkle the sugar and salt over the nuts.

8. Let the nuts cool in the refrigerator for at least 2 hours until the honey and sugar have hardened.

9. Once the honey and sugar have set, store the honey-roasted mixed nuts in an airtight container in the refrigerator.

Baked Apple

Servings: 6
Cooking Time: 20 Minutes
Ingredients:

- 3 small Honey Crisp or other baking apples
- 3 tablespoons maple syrup
- 3 tablespoons chopped pecans
- 1 tablespoon firm butter, cut into 6 pieces

Directions:

1. Pour 120 ml (1/2 cup) of water into the drawer of the air fryer.

2. Thoroughly wash and dry the apples.

3. Cut the apples in half and remove the core and a little bit of the flesh to create a hollow cavity for the pecans.

4. Place the apple halves in the air fryer basket, with the cut side facing up.

5. Spoon 7.5 ml (1.5 teaspoons) of chopped pecans into each apple's cavity.

6. Drizzle 7.5 ml (1/2 tablespoon) of maple syrup over the pecans inside each apple.

7. Top each apple half with 2.5 ml (1/2 teaspoon) of butter.

8. Cook in the air fryer at 180°C (360°F) for 20 minutes or until the apples are tender.

Baked Caramelized Peaches

Servings: 6
Cooking Time: 25 Minutes
Ingredients:

- 3 pitted peaches, halved
- 2 tablespoons brown sugar
- 240 ml heavy cream
- 1 teaspoon vanilla extract
- 1/4 teaspoon ground cinnamon
- 240 ml fresh blueberries

Directions:

1. Preheat the air fryer to 190°C (380°F).

2. Place the peach halves in the frying basket with the cut side facing up, then sprinkle them with brown sugar.

Bake for 7-11 minutes, allowing the peaches to caramelize around the edges.

3. In a mixing bowl, whisk the heavy cream, vanilla extract, and ground cinnamon until stiff peaks form.

4. Carefully fold the caramelized peaches into a serving plate.

5. Spoon the whipped cream mixture into the hollowed peach halves.

6. Top with fresh blueberries.

7. Serve and enjoy your baked caramelized peaches with a delightful cream topping and blueberries.

One-bowl Chocolate Buttermilk Cake

Servings: 6
Cooking Time: 16-20 Minutes
Ingredients:
- 90g All-purpose flour
- 100g Granulated white sugar
- 15g Unsweetened cocoa powder
- 2.5ml Baking soda
- 1.25ml Table salt
- 120ml Buttermilk
- 30ml Vegetable oil
- 3.75ml Vanilla extract
- Baking spray (for greasing)

Directions:
1. Preheat the air fryer to 160°C (or 165°C if that's the closest setting).

2. In a large bowl, stir together the flour, sugar, cocoa powder, baking soda, and salt until well combined.

3. Add the buttermilk, vegetable oil, and vanilla extract. Stir just until a thick, grainy batter forms.

4. Use baking spray to generously coat the inside of a 15cm (6-inch) round cake pan.

5. Scrape and spread the chocolate batter into the prepared pan, smoothing it out into an even layer.

6. Place the pan in the air fryer basket and air-fry undisturbed for 16 minutes for a 15cm (6-inch) layer, 18 minutes for a 18cm (7-inch) layer, or 20 minutes for a 20cm (8-inch) layer, or until a toothpick or cake tester inserted into the center of the cake comes out clean. Start checking it at the 14-minute mark to determine doneness.

7. Use oven mitts or silicone baking mitts to carefully transfer the cake pan to a wire rack. Allow it to cool for 5 minutes.

8. To unmold, place a cutting board over the cake pan and invert both the board and the pan. Lift the still-warm pan off the cake layer.

9. Set the wire rack on top of the cake layer and invert everything with the cutting board so that the cake layer is now right side up on the wire rack. Remove the cutting board.

10. Continue cooling the cake for at least 10 minutes or until it reaches room temperature, which should take about 30 minutes, before slicing it into wedges.

Maple Cinnamon Cheesecake

Servings: 4
Cooking Time: 12 Minutes
Ingredients:
- 6 sheets of cinnamon graham crackers
- 2 tablespoons butter
- 225g Neufchâtel cream cheese
- 3 tablespoons pure maple syrup
- 1 large egg
- 1/2 teaspoon ground cinnamon
- 1/4 teaspoon salt

Directions:
1. Preheat the air fryer to 180°C (350°F).

2. Place the graham crackers in a food processor and process until they are crushed into fine crumbs. Mix the crumbs with the melted butter and press the mixture into a mini air-fryer-safe pan lined with parchment paper at the bottom. Place the pan in the air fryer and cook for 4 minutes.

3. In a large bowl, combine the Neufchâtel cream cheese and maple syrup. Use a hand mixer or a stand mixer to beat them together until the mixture is smooth. Add the egg, ground cinnamon, and salt, and mix on medium speed until well combined.

4. Remove the graham cracker crust from the air fryer and pour the cheesecake batter into the pan.

5. Place the pan back in the air fryer, adjusting the temperature to 160°C (315°F). Cook for 18 minutes. Carefully remove the cheesecake when cooking is complete; the top should be lightly browned and firm.

6. Keep the cheesecake in the pan and refrigerate it for 3 hours or more to allow it to firm up before serving.

Honey-pecan Yogurt Cake

Servings: 6
Cooking Time: 18-24 Minutes
Ingredients:

- 150 grams All-purpose flour
- 1/4 teaspoon Baking powder
- 1/4 teaspoon Baking soda
- 1/4 teaspoon Table salt
- 5 tablespoons Plain full-fat, low-fat, or fat-free Greek yogurt
- 5 tablespoons Honey
- 5 tablespoons Pasteurized egg substitute, such as Egg Beaters, or use 1 whole egg
- 2 teaspoons Vanilla extract
- 70 grams Chopped pecans
- Baking spray

Directions:

1. Preheat the air fryer to 163°C (325°F) or 166°C (330°F), depending on the closest setting available.

2. In a small bowl, mix the all-purpose flour, baking powder, baking soda, and table salt until well combined.

3. In a medium bowl, using an electric hand mixer at medium speed, beat together the Greek yogurt, honey, egg substitute (or whole egg), and vanilla extract until smooth, for about 2 minutes. Be sure to scrape down the inside of the bowl once or twice.

4. Turn off the mixer and remove the beaters. Fold in the flour mixture with a rubber spatula, just until all of the flour has been moistened. Then, fold in the chopped pecans until they are evenly distributed in the mixture.

5. Use baking spray to generously coat the inside of a 6-inch round cake pan (for a small batch), a 7-inch round cake pan (for a medium batch), or an 8-inch round cake pan (for a large batch).

6. Scrape and spread the cake batter into the pan, smoothing it out to an even layer.

7. Place the cake pan in the air fryer basket and air-fry for 18 minutes (for a 6-inch layer), 22 minutes (for a 7-inch layer), or 24 minutes (for an 8-inch layer), or until a toothpick or cake tester inserted into the center of the cake comes out clean. Begin checking the cake at the 15-minute mark to determine the progress.

8. Use hot pads or silicone baking mitts to carefully transfer the cake pan to a wire rack. Allow it to cool for 5 minutes.

9. To unmold the cake, set a cutting board over the baking pan and invert both the board and the pan. Lift the still-warm pan off the cake layer. Set the wire rack on top of the cake layer and invert the whole assembly with the cutting board, so that the cake layer is now right side up on the wire rack. Remove the cutting board and continue cooling the cake for at least 10 minutes or until it reaches room temperature, which should take about 30 minutes.

10. Once the cake has cooled, you can slice it into wedges and serve.

Air-fried Beignets

Servings: 24
Cooking Time: 5 Minutes
Ingredients:

- 175ml lukewarm water (about 32°C)
- 55g sugar
- 1 generous teaspoon active dry yeast (½ envelope)
- 435g to 480g all-purpose flour
- 2.5ml salt
- 30g unsalted butter, room temperature and cut into small pieces
- 1 egg, lightly beaten
- 120ml evaporated milk
- 60g melted butter
- 125g icing sugar
- Chocolate sauce or raspberry sauce, to dip

Directions:

1. Combine the lukewarm water, a pinch of the sugar, and the yeast in a bowl and let it proof for 5 minutes. It should froth a little. If it doesn't froth, your yeast is not active and you should start again with new yeast.

2. Combine 435g of the flour, salt, 30g of butter, and the remaining sugar in a large bowl, or in the bowl of a stand mixer. Add the egg, evaporated milk, and yeast mixture to the bowl and mix with a wooden spoon (or the paddle attachment of the stand mixer) until the dough comes together in a sticky ball. Add a little more flour if necessary to get the dough to form. Transfer the dough to an oiled bowl, cover with plastic wrap or a clean kitchen towel, and let it rise in a warm place for at least 2 hours or until it has doubled in size. Longer is better for flavor development, and you can even let the dough rest in the refrigerator overnight (just remember to bring it to room temperature before proceeding with the recipe).

3. Roll the dough out to 1.25cm thickness. Cut the dough into rectangular or diamond-shaped pieces. You

can make the beignets any size you like, but this recipe will give you 24 (5cm x 7.5cm) rectangles.

4. Preheat the air fryer to 180°C (350°F).

5. Brush the beignets on both sides with some of the melted butter and air-fry in batches at 180°C (350°F) for 5 minutes, turning them over halfway through if desired. (They will brown on all sides without being flipped, but flipping them will brown them more evenly.)

6. As soon as the beignets are finished, transfer them to a plate or baking sheet and dust with the icing sugar. Serve warm with a chocolate or raspberry sauce. Enjoy!

Nutty Cookies

Servings: 6
Cooking Time: 25 Minutes
Ingredients:

- 30g pistachios
- 30g evaporated cane sugar
- 30g raw almonds
- 60g almond flour
- 5ml pure vanilla extract
- 1 egg white

Directions:

1. Preheat the air fryer to 190°C (375°F).

2. Add 30g of pistachios and 30g of almonds into a food processor. Pulse until they resemble crumbles. Roughly chop the remaining pistachios with a sharp knife.

3. Combine all the ingredients in a large bowl until they are completely incorporated.

4. Form 6 equally-sized balls from the mixture and transfer them to a parchment-lined frying basket, leaving about 2.5cm (1 inch) of space between each portion.

5. Bake for 7 minutes.

6. Cool the cookies on a wire rack for 5 minutes.

7. Serve and enjoy your Nutty Cookies.

Kiwi Pastry Bites

Servings: 6
Cooking Time: 45 Minutes
Ingredients:

- 3 kiwi fruits, cut into 12 pieces
- 12 wonton wrappers
- 120 milliliters peanut butter

Directions:

1. Lay out the wonton wrappers on a clean, flat surface.

2. Place a piece of kiwi on each wrapper, followed by 1 teaspoon of peanut butter.

3. Fold each wrapper from one corner to the opposite corner to create a triangle.

4. Bring the two bottom corners together to seal, but do not seal too tightly. Gently press out any air and then press the open edges to seal the triangle.

5. Preheat the air fryer to 190°C (370°F).

6. Grease the air fryer basket to prevent sticking.

7. Place the prepared wontons in the greased frying basket.

8. Air fry the wontons for 15-18 minutes, flipping them once halfway through cooking, or until they are golden and crisp.

9. Allow the cooked Kiwi Pastry Bites to cool for a few minutes before serving.

Chocolate Rum Brownies

Servings: 6
Cooking Time: 30 Minutes + Cooling Time
Ingredients:

- 115 grams butter, melted
- 200 grams white sugar
- 5 ml (1 teaspoon) dark rum
- 2 eggs
- 65 grams all-purpose flour
- 40 grams cocoa powder
- 1/4 teaspoon baking powder
- A pinch of salt

Directions:

1. Preheat your air fryer to 180°C (350°F).

2. In a mixing bowl, whisk together the melted butter, eggs, and dark rum until the mixture becomes slightly fluffy and all ingredients are thoroughly combined.

3. In a separate bowl, combine the all-purpose flour, white sugar, cocoa powder, baking powder, and a pinch of salt. Stir to combine the dry ingredients.

4. Gradually pour the dry ingredient mixture into the wet ingredients, stirring continuously until the batter is thoroughly blended, and there are no lumps.

5. Grease a cake pan.

6. Spoon the brownie batter into the greased cake pan, spreading it out evenly.

7. Place the cake pan into the frying basket of your air fryer.

8. Bake at 180°C (350°F) for 20 minutes, or until a toothpick inserted into the center comes out dry and clean.

9. After baking, remove the pan from the air fryer and let the brownies cool for several minutes.

10. Cut the brownies into squares or slices.

11. Serve and enjoy your delicious Chocolate Rum Brownies!

Black And Blue Clafoutis

Servings: 2
Cooking Time: 15 Minutes
Ingredients:
- 6-inch pie pan
- 3 large eggs
- 120 grams sugar
- 1 teaspoon vanilla extract
- 28 grams butter, melted
- 240 ml milk
- 60 grams all-purpose flour*
- 120 grams blackberries
- 120 grams blueberries
- 2 tablespoons icing sugar (confectioners' sugar)

Directions:
1. Preheat the air fryer to 160°C (320°F).
2. In a bowl, combine the eggs and sugar, then whisk vigorously until the mixture is smooth, lighter in color, and well combined.
3. Add the vanilla extract, melted butter, and milk to the egg-sugar mixture and whisk together thoroughly.
4. Gradually add the all-purpose flour and whisk just until no lumps or streaks of white remain.
5. Scatter half of the blueberries and blackberries in a greased 6-inch pie pan or cake pan.
6. Pour half of the batter (approximately 300 ml) over the berries.
7. Transfer the tart pan to the air fryer basket. You can use an aluminum foil sling to help with this by taking a long piece of aluminum foil, folding it in half lengthwise twice until it is roughly 66 cm by 5 cm. Place this under the pie dish and hold the ends of the foil to move the pie dish in and out of the air fryer basket. Tuck the ends of the foil beside the pie dish while it cooks in the air fryer.
8. Air-fry at 160°C (320°F) for 15 minutes or until the clafoutis has puffed up and is still slightly jiggly in the center.

9. Remove the clafoutis from the air fryer, invert it onto a plate, and let it cool while you bake the second batch.
10. Serve the clafoutis warm, dusted with icing sugar on top.

Cheese & Honey Stuffed Figs

Servings: 4
Cooking Time: 15 Minutes
Ingredients:
- 8 figs, stem off
- 55 grams cottage cheese
- 1.25 ml ground cinnamon
- 1.25 ml orange zest
- 1.25 ml vanilla extract
- 30 ml honey
- 15 ml olive oil

Directions:
1. Preheat the air fryer to 180°C (360°F).
2. Cut an "X" in the top of each fig 1/3 way through, leaving intact the base.
3. Mix together the cottage cheese, cinnamon, orange zest, vanilla extract, and 15 ml of honey in a bowl.
4. Spoon the cheese mixture into the cavity of each fig.
5. Put the figs in a single layer in the frying basket. Drizzle the olive oil over the top of the figs and roast for 10 minutes.
6. Drizzle with the remaining honey.

Carrot Cake With Cream Cheese Icing

Servings: 6
Cooking Time: 55 Minutes
Ingredients:
- 190 grams all-purpose flour
- 5 grams baking powder
- 2.5 grams baking soda
- 2.5 grams ground cinnamon
- 0.5 grams ground nutmeg
- 1 gram salt
- 300 grams grated carrot (about 3 to 4 medium carrots or 2 large)
- 150 grams granulated sugar
- 60 grams brown sugar
- 2 eggs
- 180 ml canola or vegetable oil

- For the icing:
- 225 grams cream cheese, softened at room temperature
- 115 grams butter (4 ounces or 1 stick), softened at room temperature
- 125 grams powdered sugar
- 5 ml pure vanilla extract

Directions:

1. Grease a 7-inch cake pan.

2. Combine the flour, baking powder, baking soda, cinnamon, nutmeg, and salt in a bowl. Add the grated carrots and toss well.

3. In a separate bowl, beat the sugars and eggs together until light and frothy. Drizzle in the oil, beating constantly.

4. Fold the egg mixture into the dry ingredients until everything is just combined, and you no longer see any traces of flour.

5. Pour the batter into the cake pan and wrap the pan completely in greased aluminum foil.

6. Preheat the air fryer to 175°C (350°F).

7. Lower the cake pan into the air fryer basket using a sling made of aluminum foil (fold a piece of aluminum foil into a strip about 5 cm wide by 60 cm long). Fold the ends of the aluminum foil into the air fryer, letting them rest on top of the cake.

8. Air-fry for 40 minutes. Remove the aluminum foil cover and air-fry for an additional 15 minutes or until a skewer inserted into the center of the cake comes out clean, and the top is nicely browned.

9. While the cake is cooking, beat the cream cheese, butter, powdered sugar, and vanilla extract together using a hand mixer, stand mixer, or food processor (or a lot of elbow grease!).

10. Remove the cake pan from the air fryer and let the cake cool in the cake pan for 10 minutes or so. Then remove the cake from the pan and let it continue to cool completely.

11. Frost the cake with the cream cheese icing and serve.

Homemade Chips Ahoy Cookies

Servings: 4
Cooking Time: 20 Minutes

Ingredients:

- 1 tablespoon coconut oil, melted
- 1 tablespoon honey
- 1 tablespoon milk
- 1/2 teaspoon vanilla extract
- 30 grams oat flour
- 2 tablespoons coconut sugar
- 1/4 teaspoon salt
- 1/4 teaspoon baking powder
- 2 tablespoons chocolate chips

Directions:

1. In a bowl, combine the melted coconut oil, honey, milk, and vanilla extract.

2. Add the oat flour, coconut sugar, salt, and baking powder to the wet ingredients. Stir until all the ingredients are well combined.

3. Add the chocolate chips to the dough and mix them in evenly.

4. Preheat the air fryer to 175°C (350°F).

5. Grease a baking pan suitable for the air fryer.

6. Drop spoonfuls of cookie dough onto the greased baking pan, leaving a little space in between each cookie.

7. Bake in the preheated air fryer for approximately 7 minutes or until the cookies turn golden brown. Be careful not to overcook.

8. Remove the cookies from the air fryer and transfer them to a cooling rack to cool.

9. Serve your Homemade Chips Ahoy cookies chilled.

Grilled Pineapple Dessert

Servings: 4
Cooking Time: 12 Minutes

Ingredients:

- Oil for misting or cooking spray
- 4 slices of fresh pineapple, each about 1.25 centimeters (1/2 inch) thick, core removed
- 1 tablespoon honey
- 1/4 teaspoon brandy
- 2 tablespoons slivered almonds, toasted
- Vanilla frozen yogurt or coconut sorbet

Directions:

1. Spray both sides of the pineapple slices with oil or cooking spray.

2. Place the pineapple slices on the grill plate or directly into the air fryer basket.

3. Cook at 200°C (390°F) for 6 minutes. Turn the slices over and cook for an additional 6 minutes.

4. While the pineapple is cooking, mix together the honey and brandy in a small bowl.

5. Remove the cooked pineapple slices from the air fryer, sprinkle them with toasted almonds, and drizzle them with the honey and brandy mixture.

6. Serve each slice of grilled pineapple with a scoop of frozen yogurt or sorbet on the side.

Choco-granola Bars With Cranberries

Servings: 6

Cooking Time: 20 Minutes

Ingredients:

- 2 tablespoons dark chocolate chunks
- 200 grams quick oats
- 2 tablespoons dried cranberries
- 3 tablespoons shredded coconut
- 120 ml maple syrup
- 1 teaspoon ground cinnamon
- 1/8 teaspoon salt
- 2 tablespoons smooth peanut butter

Directions:

1. Preheat your air fryer to 180°C (360°F).

2. In a mixing bowl, combine the quick oats, dried cranberries, shredded coconut, dark chocolate chunks, ground cinnamon, and salt.

3. In a separate microwave-safe bowl, heat the maple syrup and peanut butter together until they are well combined. This should take about 30 seconds in the microwave. Stir the mixture until smooth.

4. Pour the warm maple syrup and peanut butter mixture over the dry ingredients. Stir thoroughly until all the ingredients are well coated and the mixture is evenly combined.

5. Line a baking pan with parchment paper, ensuring that the paper hangs over the edges for easy removal later.

6. Transfer the granola mixture into the parchment-lined baking pan and press it down firmly into a single, even layer.

7. Place the baking pan into the frying basket of your air fryer.

8. Air fry at 180°C (360°F) for 15 minutes. Make sure to check it periodically to prevent overcooking.

9. After air frying, carefully remove the pan from the fryer. Use the edges of the parchment paper to lift the granola cake out of the pan.

10. Allow the granola cake to cool for about 5 minutes.

11. Once cooled, slice it into bars or squares.

12. Serve and enjoy your Choco-Granola Bars with Cranberries!

Fall Pumpkin Cake

Servings: 6

Cooking Time: 50 Minutes

Ingredients:

- For the Crust:
- 75 grams pecan pieces
- 5 gingersnap cookies
- 75 grams light brown sugar
- 85 grams butter, melted
- For the Cake:
- 3 eggs
- 1/2 teaspoon vanilla extract
- 240 grams pumpkin purée
- 2 tablespoons sour cream
- 65 grams all-purpose flour
- 30 grams tapioca flour
- 1/2 teaspoon cornstarch
- 100 grams granulated sugar
- 1/2 teaspoon baking soda
- 1 teaspoon baking powder
- 1 teaspoon pumpkin pie spice
- For the Mascarpone Frosting:
- 170 grams mascarpone cheese
- 150 grams powdered sugar
- 1 teaspoon cinnamon
- 30 grams butter, softened
- 15 ml milk
- For Garnish:
- 15 grams flaked almonds

Directions:

1. In a food processor, blitz the pecan pieces, gingersnap cookies, light brown sugar, and 85 grams of melted butter until well combined. Press this mixture into the bottom of a lightly greased cake pan.

2. Preheat your air fryer to 180°C (350°F).

3. In a bowl, whisk together the eggs, remaining melted butter, 1/2 teaspoon of vanilla extract, pumpkin purée, and sour cream.

4. In another bowl, combine the all-purpose flour, tapioca flour, cornstarch, granulated sugar, baking soda, baking powder, and pumpkin pie spice.

5. Add the wet ingredients to the dry ingredients and combine, being careful not to overmix.

6. Pour the cake batter into the prepared cake pan and cover it with aluminum foil.

7. Place the cake pan in the air fryer basket and bake for 30 minutes. Then, remove the foil and cook for an additional 5 minutes or until a toothpick inserted into the center comes out clean.

8. Allow the cake to cool on a wire rack for 10 minutes, then carefully turn it onto a large serving platter.

9. In a small bowl, whisk together the mascarpone cheese, powdered sugar, remaining 1/2 teaspoon of vanilla extract, cinnamon, softened butter, and milk.

10. Spread the mascarpone frosting over the cooled cake and garnish with flaked almonds.

11. Cut the Fall Pumpkin Cake into slices and serve.

Banana Fritters

Servings: 6
Cooking Time: 20 Minutes
Ingredients:
- 1 egg
- 30 grams cornstarch
- 30 grams bread crumbs
- 3 bananas, halved crosswise
- 60 ml caramel sauce

Directions:
1. Preheat the air fryer to 175°C (350°F).
2. Set up three small bowls. In the first bowl, add the cornstarch. In the second bowl, beat the egg. In the third bowl, add the bread crumbs.
3. Dip the banana halves in the cornstarch first, then the egg, and then dredge them in bread crumbs.
4. Place the coated banana halves in the greased frying basket and spray them with oil.
5. Air fry for 8 minutes, flipping them once around the 5-minute mark.
6. Remove the banana fritters to a serving plate and drizzle them with caramel sauce.
7. Serve warm and enjoy your banana fritters!

Nutty Banana Bread

Servings: 6
Cooking Time: 30 Minutes
Ingredients:
- 2 bananas

- 30g ground flaxseed
- 60ml milk
- 15ml apple cider vinegar
- 15ml vanilla extract
- 2.5ml ground cinnamon
- 30ml honey
- 60g oat flour
- 2.5ml baking soda
- 45g butter

Directions:
1. Preheat the air fryer to 160°C (320°F).
2. Using a fork, mash the bananas until they are chunky.
3. Mix in the ground flaxseed, milk, apple cider vinegar, vanilla extract, cinnamon, and honey.
4. Finally, toss in the oat flour and baking soda, stirring until the mixture is smooth but still chunky.
5. Divide the batter between 6 cupcake molds.
6. Top each with one and a half teaspoons of butter and swirl it slightly.
7. Bake for 18 minutes until the banana bread is golden brown and puffy.
8. Let the banana bread cool completely before serving.

Guilty Chocolate Cookies

Servings: 6
Cooking Time: 25 Minutes
Ingredients:
- 3 eggs, beaten
- 1 teaspoon vanilla extract
- 1 teaspoon apple cider vinegar
- 75 grams butter, softened
- 75 grams sugar
- 30 grams cacao powder
- 1/4 teaspoon baking soda

Directions:
1. Preheat the air fryer to 150°C (300°F).
2. In a bowl, combine the beaten eggs, vanilla extract, and apple cider vinegar until well combined. Refrigerate this mixture for 5 minutes.
3. Whisk in the softened butter and sugar until you get a smooth mixture.
4. Finally, add the cacao powder and baking soda to the mixture and continue whisking until the batter is smooth.
5. Form the batter into balls and place them onto a parchment-lined frying basket in the air fryer.

6. Bake for 13 minutes or until the cookies are browned.

7. Using a fork, gently flatten each cookie.

8. Let the cookies cool completely before serving.

Lemon Iced Donut Balls

Servings: 6

Cooking Time: 25 Minutes

Ingredients:

- 1 can jumbo biscuit dough
- 10 milliliters lemon juice
- 60 grams icing sugar, sifted

Directions:

1. Preheat the air fryer to 182°C (360°F).

2. Divide the biscuit dough into 16 equal portions.

3. Roll each portion of dough into balls with a thickness of about 1.5 inches.

4. Place the dough balls (donut holes) in the greased frying basket of the air fryer.

5. Air fry the donut holes for 8 minutes, flipping them once during cooking to ensure even browning.

6. While the donut holes are cooking, mix the sifted icing sugar and lemon juice together until you have a smooth icing.

7. Once the donut holes are done, remove them from the air fryer.

8. Spread the lemon icing over the top of the donut holes.

9. Allow the icing to set for a bit.

10. Serve your Lemon Iced Donut Balls.

Banana-lemon Bars

Servings: 6

Cooking Time: 40 Minutes

Ingredients:

- 175 grams flour
- 30 grams powdered sugar
- 60 ml coconut oil, melted
- 100 grams brown sugar
- 1 tablespoon lemon zest
- 60 ml lemon juice
- 1/8 teaspoon salt
- 60 grams mashed bananas
- 1¾ teaspoons cornstarch
- ¾ teaspoon baking powder

Directions:

1. Combine the flour, powdered sugar, and melted coconut oil in a bowl. Place the mixture in the fridge to chill.

2. In another bowl, mix together the brown sugar, lemon zest, lemon juice, salt, mashed bananas, cornstarch, and baking powder. Stir until well combined.

3. Preheat the air fryer to 175°C (350°F).

4. Spray a baking pan with oil.

5. Remove the chilled crust mixture from the fridge and press it into the bottom of the prepared pan to form a crust.

6. Place the pan in the air fryer and bake for 5 minutes or until the crust is firm.

7. Remove the pan from the air fryer and spread the lemon filling over the crust.

8. Bake for an additional 18-20 minutes or until the top is golden.

9. Allow the bars to cool for an hour in the fridge.

10. Once firm and cooled, cut into pieces and serve.

Coconut Macaroons

Servings: 12

Cooking Time: 8 Minutes

Ingredients:

- 160 grams shredded sweetened coconut
- 11 grams flour
- 25 grams sugar
- 1 egg white
- 2.5 ml (1/2 teaspoon) almond extract

Directions:

1. Preheat your air fryer to 165°C (330°F).

2. In a mixing bowl, combine the shredded sweetened coconut, flour, sugar, egg white, and almond extract. Mix all the ingredients together until well combined.

3. Shape the coconut mixture into 12 small balls.

4. Place all 12 macaroons in the air fryer basket. They won't expand, so you can place them close together, but make sure they don't touch.

5. Cook the macaroons in the air fryer at 165°C (330°F) for 8 minutes or until they turn golden brown.

6. Once done, remove the Coconut Macaroons from the air fryer and let them cool slightly.

7. Enjoy your Coconut Macaroons!

Berry Streusel Cake

Servings: 6
Cooking Time: 60 Minutes
Ingredients:
- 2 tablespoons demerara sugar
- 2 tablespoons sunflower oil
- 30 grams almond flour
- 120 grams pastry flour
- 100 grams brown sugar
- 1 teaspoon baking powder
- 1 tablespoon lemon zest
- 1/4 teaspoon salt
- 180 ml milk
- 30 ml olive oil
- 1 teaspoon vanilla extract
- 150 grams blueberries
- 60 grams powdered sugar
- 1 tablespoon lemon juice
- 1/8 teaspoon salt

Directions:
1. In a bowl, mix the demerara sugar, sunflower oil, and almond flour, then place it in the refrigerator to chill.
2. In another bowl, whisk together the pastry flour, brown sugar, baking powder, lemon zest, and salt.
3. Add the milk, olive oil, and vanilla extract to the dry ingredients and stir with a rubber spatula until well combined.
4. Gently fold in the blueberries.
5. Coat the inside of a baking pan with oil and pour the batter into the pan.
6. Preheat the air fryer to 155°C (310°F).
7. Remove the almond mixture from the fridge and spread it evenly over the cake batter.
8. Place the cake in the air fryer and bake for 45 minutes or until a knife inserted in the center comes out clean and the top is golden.
9. In a bowl, combine the powdered sugar, lemon juice, and salt to make the icing.
10. Once the cake has cooled, slice it into 4 pieces and drizzle each slice with the icing.
11. Serve and enjoy your Berry Streusel Cake!

Blueberry Cheesecake Tartlets

Servings: 9
Cooking Time: 6 Minutes
Ingredients:
- 225 grams cream cheese, softened
- 60 grams sugar
- 1 egg
- 1/2 teaspoon vanilla extract
- Zest of 2 lemons, divided
- 9 mini graham cracker tartlet shells*
- 340 grams blueberries
- 1/2 teaspoon ground cinnamon
- Juice of 1/2 lemon
- 60 grams apricot preserves

Directions:
1. Preheat the air fryer to 165°C (330°F).
2. In a medium bowl, combine the softened cream cheese, sugar, egg, vanilla extract, and the zest of one lemon. Blend until smooth using a hand mixer or by hand.
3. Pour the cream cheese mixture into the mini graham cracker tartlet shells.
4. Air-fry 3 tartlets at a time at 165°C (330°F) for 6 minutes, rotating them in the air fryer basket halfway through the cooking time.
5. In a separate bowl, combine the blueberries, ground cinnamon, zest of one lemon, and the juice of half a lemon.
6. Melt the apricot preserves in the microwave or over low heat in a saucepan. Pour the melted preserves over the blueberries and gently toss to coat.
7. Allow the cheesecake tartlets to cool completely, and then top each one with a portion of the blueberry mixture.
8. Garnish the tartlets with a little sugared lemon peel if desired and refrigerate until you are ready to serve.

APPENDIX A: Measurement

BASIC KITCHEN CONVERSIONS & EQUIVALENTS DRY MEASUREMENTS CONVERSION CHART

3 TEASPOONS = 1 TABLESPOON = 1/16 CUP

6 TEASPOONS = 2 TABLESPOONS = 1/8 CUP

12 TEASPOONS = 4 TABLESPOONS = 1/4 CUP

24 TEASPOONS = 8 TABLESPOONS = 1/2 CUP

36 TEASPOONS = 12 TABLESPOONS = 3/4 CUP

48 TEASPOONS = 16 TABLESPOONS = 1 CUP

METRIC TO US COOKING CONVERSIONS OVEN TEMPERATURES

120 ° C = 250 ° F 160 ° C = 320 ° F 180° C = 350 ° F 205 ° C = 400 ° F 220 ° C = 425 ° F

LIQUID MEASUREMENTS CONVERSION CHART

8 FLUID OUNCES = 1 CUP = 1/2 PINT = 1/4 QUART

16 FLUID OUNCES = 2 CUPS = 1 PINT = 1/2 QUART

32 FLUID OUNCES = 4 CUPS = 2 PINTS = 1 QUART = 1/4 GALLON

128 FLUID OUNCES = 16 CUPS = 8 PINTS = 4 QUARTS = 1 GALLON

BAKING IN GRAMS

1 CUP FLOUR = 140 GRAMS

1 CUP SUGAR = 150 GRAMS

1 CUP POWDERED SUGAR = 160 GRAMS

1 CUP HEAVY CREAM = 235 GRAMS

VOLUME

1 MILLILITER = 1/5 TEASPOON

5 ML = 1 TEASPOON

15 ML = 1 TABLESPOON

240 ML = 1 CUP OR 8 FLUID OUNCES

1 LITER = 34 FL. OUNCES

WEIGHT

1 GRAM = .035 OUNCES

100 GRAMS = 3.5 OUNCES

500 GRAMS = 1.1 POUNDS

1 KILOGRAM = 35 OUNCES

US TO METRIC COOKING CONVERSIONS

1/5 TSP = 1 ML

1 TSP = 5 ML

1 TBSP = 15 ML

1 FL OUNCE = 30 ML

1 CUP = 237 ML

1 PINT (2 CUPS) = 473 ML

1 QUART (4 CUPS) = .95 LITER

1 GALLON (16 CUPS) = 3.8 LITERS

1 OZ = 28 GRAMS

1 POUND = 454 GRAMS

BUTTER

1 CUP BUTTER = 2 STICKS = 8 OUNCES = 230 GRAMS = 8 TABLESPOONS

WHAT DOES 1 CUP EQUAL

1 CUP = 8 FLUID OUNCES

1 CUP = 16 TABLESPOONS

1 CUP = 48 TEASPOONS

1 CUP = 1/2 PINT

1 CUP = 1/4 QUART

1 CUP = 1/16 GALLON

1 CUP = 240 ML

BAKING PAN CONVERSIONS

1 CUP ALL-PURPOSE FLOUR = 4.5 OZ

1 CUP ROLLED OATS = 3 OZ 1 LARGE EGG = 1.7 OZ

1 CUP BUTTER = 8 OZ 1 CUP MILK = 8 OZ

1 CUP HEAVY CREAM = 8.4 OZ

1 CUP GRANULATED SUGAR = 7.1 OZ

1 CUP PACKED BROWN SUGAR = 7.75 OZ

1 CUP VEGETABLE OIL = 7.7 OZ

1 CUP UNSIFTED POWDERED SUGAR = 4.4 OZ

BAKING PAN CONVERSIONS

9-INCH ROUND CAKE PAN = 12 CUPS

10-INCH TUBE PAN =16 CUPS

11-INCH BUNDT PAN = 12 CUPS

9-INCH SPRINGFORM PAN = 10 CUPS

9 X 5 INCH LOAF PAN = 8 CUPS

9-INCH SQUARE PAN = 8 CUPS

APPENDIX B: Recipes Index

Bite-sized Blooming Onions 52
Black And Blue Clafoutis 94
Black Bean Veggie Burgers 77
Black Olive & Shrimp Salad 42
Black-olive Poppers 31
Blanket Breakfast Eggs 14
Blistered Shishito Peppers 32
Blooming Onion 28
Blueberry & Lemon Breakfast Muffins 21
Blueberry Cheesecake Tartlets 99
Blueberry Crisp 88
Bocconcini Balls 15
Boss Chicken Cobb Salad 70
Breaded Avocado Tacos 59
Breaded Parmesan Perch 42
Breaded Pork Chops 37
Breakfast Doughnuts 19
Breakfast Eggs & Spinach 20
Breakfast Sausage Burgers 14
Brie-currant & Bacon Spread 31
British Fish & Chips 48
Buffalo Bites 29
Buffalo Cauliflower 26
Buffalo Chicken Wings 24
Buttered Swordfish Steaks 52
Buttermilk Pork Chops 35
Buttery Lobster Tails 49
Buttery Spiced Pecans 25

C

Cajun Chicken Kebabs 70
Cajun Flounder Fillets 42
Cajun-seasoned Shrimp 49
Cajun-spiced Pickle Chips 24
Cal-mex Turkey Patties 75
Carrot Cake With Cream Cheese Icing 94
Catalan Sardines With Romesco Sauce 45
Cayenne-spiced Roasted Pecans 22
Char Siu Buffalo 36
Cheddar Stuffed Pepper 24
Cheddar Stuffed Portobellos With Salsa 63
Cheddar-bean Flautas 59
Cheese & Ham Sliders 35
Cheese & Honey Stuffed Figs 94
Cheese Ravioli 55
Cheese Scones 19
Cheeseburger Egg Rolls 35

Cheesy Chicken Tenders 73

Cheesy Eggplant Lasagna 61

Cheesy Eggplant Rounds 54

Cheesy Meatballs 40

Cheesy Salmon-stuffed Avocados 41

Cheesy Sausage Breakfast Pockets 17

Cheesy Tuna Tower 45

Cheesy Veggie Frittata 61

Cherry Chipotle Bbq Chicken Wings 27

Chewy Coconut Cake 88

Chicken And Cheese Chimichangas 66

Chicken And Wheat Stir Fry 69

Chicken Apple Brie Melt 79

Chicken Breasts Wrapped In Bacon 65

Chicken Burgers With Blue Cheese Sauce 76

Chicken Club Sandwiches 81

Chicken Cordon Bleu 69

Chicken Gyros 83

Chicken Kiev 75

Chicken Milanese 75

Chicken Saltimbocca Sandwiches 86

Chicken Spiedies 79

Chicken Wellington 69

Chilean-style Chicken Empanadas 71

Chili Cheese Dogs 87

Chinese Fish Noodle Bowls 44

Chipotle Sunflower Seeds 25

Chive Potato Pierogi 55

Choco-granola Bars With Cranberries 96

Chocolate Rum Brownies 93

Cinnamon Apple Crisps 22

Classic Chicken Cobb Salad 73

Coconut Curry Chicken With Coconut Rice 66

Coconut Jerk Shrimp 43

Coconut Macaroons 98

Coconut Shrimp With Plum Sauce 47

Corn And Pepper Jack Chile Rellenos With Roasted Tomato Sauce 60

Courgette Fries 16

Crispy Chicken Parmesan 72

Crispy Cordon Bleu 67

Crunchy Falafel Balls 86

Crunchy Mexican Breakfast Wrap 18

Cumin Shoestring Carrots 17

Curried Cauliflower 63

D

Delicious Breakfast Casserole 20
Dijon Thyme Burgers 80

E

Easy Asian-style Tuna 50
Easy Cheese & Bacon Toasties 16
Effortless Mac 'n' Cheese 57
Eggplant Parmesan 53
Eggplant Parmesan Subs 84
Enchilada Chicken Quesadillas 72
European Pancakes 20

F

Falafel 53
Fall Pumpkin Cake 96
Family Chicken Fingers 72
Fennel & Chicken Ratatouille 65
Fennel Tofu Bites 56
Fillet Mignon Wrapped In Bacon 39
Fish And "chips" 48
Fish Nuggets With Broccoli Dip 43
French Grouper Nicoise 51
French Toast 17
French Toast Slices 21
Fried Scallops 50
Fried Twinkies 89

G

Garlic-butter Lobster Tails 46
Garlic-herb Pita Chips 33
Golden Fried Tofu 58
Grain-free Chicken Katsu 67
Grilled Pineapple Dessert 95
Guilty Chocolate Cookies 97

H

Halloumi Fries 21
Hard Boiled Eggs Air Fryer Style 19
Harissa Chicken Wings 67
Herbed Cheese Brittle 28
Holiday Lobster Salad 47
Holiday Shrimp Scampi 51

Homemade Chips Ahoy Cookies 95
Homemade Crispy Pepperoni Pizza 34
Homemade Pretzel Bites 25
Home-style Taro Chips 27
Honey Pear Chips 59
Honey Pecan Shrimp 44
Honey-mustard Chicken Wings 27
Honey-pecan Yogurt Cake 92
Honey-roasted Mixed Nuts 90
Hungarian Spiralized Fries 22

I

Inside Out Cheeseburgers 85
Inside-out Cheeseburgers 82
Intense Buffalo Chicken Wings 66
Italian Meatballs 33
Italian-style Fried Cauliflower 57

J

Japanese Pork Chops 39
Japanese-inspired Glazed Chicken 74

K

Kale & Lentils With Crispy Onions 54
Kiwi Pastry Bites 93

L

Lamb Burgers 39
Lamb Calzone 39
Lemon Herb Whole Cornish Hen 68
Lemon Iced Donut Balls 98
Lime Halibut Parcels 46
Loaded Hash Browns 14

M

Mahi Mahi With Cilantro-chili Butter 47
Mahi-mahi "burrito" Fillets 48
Maple Balsamic Glazed Salmon 51
Maple Cinnamon Cheesecake 91
Meatless Kimchi Bowls 61
Meatloaf 38
Meaty Egg Cups 14
Mexican Breakfast Burritos 20

Mexican Cheeseburgers 85
Mini Carrot Cakes 88
Morning Sausage Wraps 15
Mozzarella Stuffed Mushrooms 30
Mushroom Bolognese Casserole 55
Mustard Glazed Pork 35
Mustard Pork Tenderloin 38

N

Nutty Banana Bread 97
Nutty Cookies 93

O

Old Fashioned Steak 38
One-bowl Chocolate Buttermilk Cake 91
Oozing Baked Eggs 18

P

Patatas Bravas 19
Perfect Burgers 80
Philly Cheesesteak Sandwiches 83
Pizza Dogs 38
Pizza Margherita With Spinach 60
Pork Chops With Honey 36
Pork With Chinese 5 Spice 39
Provolone Stuffed Meatballs 83
Pulled Pork, Bacon, And Cheese Sliders 33

Q

Quick Chicken Nuggets 71
Quick-to-make Quesadillas 53
Quinoa & Black Bean Stuffed Peppers 58

R

Raspberry Breakfast Pockets 18
Reuben Sandwiches 84
Rice & Bean Burritos 64
Rigatoni With Roasted Onions, Fennel, Spinach, And Lemon Pepper Ricotta 56
Roast Beef 34
Roast Pork 37
Roasted Vegetable Lasagna 62

S

Salmon Burgers 85
Salt And Pepper Belly Pork 34
Sausage And Pepper Subs 82
Southern Style Pork Chops 37
Spiced Vegetable Galette 62
Steak And Mushrooms 37

T

Tahini Beef Bites 36
Thai-style Pork Sliders 79
Thanksgiving Turkey Sandwiches 81
Toad In The Hole, Breakfast Style 16
Traditional Pork Chops 40
Turkey And Mushroom Burgers 74
Turkey Burgers 78

V

Vegan Avocado Fries 30

W

White Bean Veggie Burgers 78
Whole Mini Peppers 18

Y

Your Favourite Breakfast Bacon 15

Printed in Great Britain
by Amazon